COOPER

Stirling Moss had just taken the lead late into the 1959 Dutch GP when, as so often happened in 1959, the Colotti gearbox on his Rob Walker Cooper failed. That allowed Jo Bonnier to go on to score BRM's first World Championship victory. Even Moss fans, who felt for their hero, cheered BRM's triumph.

COOPER

MIKE LAWRENCE

FOREWORD BY JOHN COOPER

SUTTON PUBLISHING

Sutton Publishing Limited
Phoenix Mill · Thrupp · Stroud
Gloucestershire · GL5 2BU

First published 1999

Title page: Jack Brabham in the 1957
International Trophy, see p. 66.
Half-title page: Mike Hawthorn in his
Cooper-Bristol at Ibsley, 1952, see p. 33.

British Library Cataloguing in Publication Data
A catalogue record for this book is available from the
British Library.

ISBN 0-7509-2344-X

Typeset in 10.5/13.5 Photina.
Typesetting and origination by
Sutton Publishing Limited.
Printed in Great Britain by
The Cromwell Press, Trowbridge, Wiltshire.

ACKNOWLEDGEMENTS

The compilation of this book would not have been possible without the help of Ted Walker of
Ferret Fotographics who provided the majority of the photographs from his extensive collection.
We are very grateful to him. Pictures were also generously supplied by John Cooper (pp. 4, 6, 40,
108, 132, 145, 158), the Indianapolis Motor Speedway Corporation (pp. 110, 111), the LAT
Archive (pp. 59, 86), the Geoff Goddard Collection (p. 48) and the Rover Group (p. 157).

When John Cooper was eight, his father built him a miniature car with a Francis-Barnett motor cycle engine
which ran on wheels normally used on the front of delivery bicycles. Charlie Cooper is at the wheel of John's car
as he takes on the Alfa Romeo Monza of his prewar partner, 'Ginger' Hamilton.

CONTENTS

John Cooper inducts son, Mike, in the mysteries of the racing car. Mike now runs John Cooper Garages in Sussex.

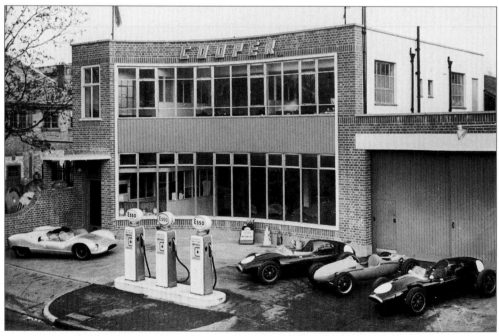

The exterior of the Cooper works in Hollyfield Road, Surbiton, in early 1959. On the left is the prototype Cooper Monaco while, on the right, are the works F1/2 cars flanking a Mk XII 500cc car, one of the last to be made. Esso was one of Cooper's principle trade supporters so, naturally, Cooper was proud to sell its fine petroleum products.

FOREWORD

by John Cooper

It is more than thirty years since there was a Cooper works racing team, but we seem to be busier than ever. The popularity of Historic racing has seen Cooper formula and sports cars return to the track with, I am happy to say, no little success.

The revival of the Mini Cooper by Rover Group and the special Mini Coopers we make at John Cooper Garages have kept us pretty busy as well. On top of that, at the time of writing, we are waiting for the Mini's successor, which will also be made in Cooper, and Cooper 'S' versions. I've been lucky enough to drive one of the prototypes and can say that it captures the spirit of the original.

It all seems a long way from the time that my father and I designed and built a 500cc single-seater to go racing and hill climbing on a budget. That simple car led us to Formula One and two World Championships.

My old friend, Mike Lawrence, has told the story in his usual entertaining and knowledgeable way. It seems unbelievable now that we won World Championships on a budget of £10,000. Even taking inflation into account that would not keep a modern team's mobile home going for a season today. Not that we had mobile homes or even, most of the time, transporters. We used to tow our Grand Prix cars to circuits on trailers, yet the racing was as fierce and we had some of the greatest drivers in history in our cars. Among them were Jack Brabham, Tony Brooks, Peter Collins, Mike Hawthorn, Phil Hill, Bruce McLaren, Stirling Moss, Jochen Rindt, Jackie Stewart and John Surtees. And there were others who bought cars from us who also made their mark in motor racing – Ken Tyrrell springs to mind, as do Bernie Ecclestone, Briggs Cunningham, Carroll Shelby and Roger Penske.

Racing is different today, of course, but then racing was different when we were involved to how it had been for my father's generation. It has been great to relive some of the fun – and frustration – of the days when Cooper Cars was active and I can only hope that readers enjoy sharing the memories.

John Cooper
Ferring
Sussex
September 1999

Steve Neal's 1968 works Mini Cooper still looks like the sort of car you could see in any high street. Sponsorship was permitted from the beginning of 1968 but had yet to filter down to saloon cars so the decals indicate trade support. Successful drivers would earn bonuses from the companies featured on the car.

Jack Brabham's Cooper T41 on its way to fourth place in the Glover Trophy (for F1 cars) at the 1957 Easter Monday meeting. Jack used to hunch over the steering wheel and hang out the tail of his car. Some thought his driving style crude, but he won three World Championships and was still winning races in 1970, his last season.

COOPER – AT A GLANCE

In this brief overview of Cooper landmarks, the main type numbers are put in brackets. The designations of the early cars were made in retrospect – T1 was given to the Austin 7 special built by Charlie Cooper for John in 1936. Not all types are recorded. The Cooper T8, for example, was a trailer, and T9 was a stretched Mk III chassis to accommodate the larger 998cc JAP engine and increased fuel capacity.

1946   Cooper builds first two 500cc cars for John Cooper (T2) and Eric Brandon (T3).

1947   Cooper builds first sports car (T4) based on 500cc chassis, but with enveloping body and 650cc Triumph engine. It is used in hill climbs, but is sold after after the engine blows up.
Eric Brandon wins first-ever 500cc race, at Gransden Lodge, in a meeting organised by the Cambridge University Automobile Club.

1948   Cooper lays down run of seven Mk II (T5) production cars, six with 500cc engines and one, for John Cooper, with a 998cc V-twin JAP unit. One of the 500cc cars is bought by Stirling Moss.
First of front-engined sports cars (T6) is built over the winter of 1948/9.

1949   Mk III Coopers (T7) with 998cc JAP engines begin to appear in International events at home and abroad. Nineteen of the forty entries for the 500cc race at the British Grand Prix meeting are Coopers.
The FIA announces that, from 1950, the 500cc category will become Formula Three.

1950   Coopers dominate the new Formula Three, winning every important race in Britain and on the Continent. Moss wins the support race at the Monaco Grand Prix. In the Grand Prix itself, Harry Schell enters his 998cc car – it is the first that a Cooper runs in a World Championship race.
First batch of customer front-engined sports cars (T14). Customers are responsible for the power unit and bodywork, and most choose an MG engine.

1951   Ecurie Richmond Cooper Mk Vs (T11) of Alan Brown and Eric Brandon win both main British Formula Three Championships.
Cooper takes international speed records with streamlined Mk V (T17).

1952   Cooper-Bristol Mk I (T20) introduced in spectacular manner by Mike Hawthorn who establishes himself as a major talent. Before the end of the year he will sign for Ferrari.
The 2-litre Formula Two is the World Championship category and Alan Brown wins Cooper's first points.
Batch of revised front-engined sports cars (T21) is made.
Cooper continues to dominate Formula Three except when Don Parker and his modified Kieft is present.

A Cooper-MG at Castle Combe during a test day, March 1953.

1953   Cooper makes Bristol-engined sports car (T22) while many of the Mk I Formula Two cars are converted into sports models by their owners.
Mk II Formula Two car (T23) is fitted with various engines, but is not a noticeable improvement over the Mk II. Other outfits, however, have made large strides forward.

1954   Cooper-Jaguar Mk I (T33) is built for Peter Whitehead, and two others are made, but they are out-classed in international racing.
The year is largely unfruitful for British cars. Cooper still dominates Formula Three, but the category has importance only in Britain. Though international interest has waned, Formula Three continues to be an important training ground in the UK. Les Leston wins the British F3 Championship for Cooper.
Cooper builds chassis for prototype Vanwall. At Tony Vandervell's request, it is a close copy of a Ferrari 375 chassis.

1955   Cooper-Jaguar Mk II (T38) is introduced and three are made. It is no more successful than the Mk I at international level.
Central-seat, mid-engined, Climax-engined 'Manx Tail' sports car (T39) is introduced and is very successful in 1100cc and 1500cc form.
A Bristol-engined 'Manx Tail' is run by Jack Brabham in the British Grand Prix.
Cooper makes its first appearance at Le Mans.
Jim Russell wins the British Formula Three Championship in a Cooper, it is the first leg of what will be a hat-trick.

1956   'Manx Tail' has to defer to new Lotus Eleven in 1100cc sports car racing, which has become the most popular class for the aspiring young driver. Cooper still dominates Formula Three, but the class is rapidly declining in popularity.

First car for forthcoming 1500cc Formula Two (T41) is made by Cooper and it runs in F2 races organised in anticipation of the new formula.

1957   Production version of F2 car (T43) is sold in unprecedented numbers for the category.

Tony Brooks wins first official 1500cc Formula Two race for Cooper and Cooper wins all but two F2 races.

Works cars, fitted with 1500cc and 1960cc engines, are run for Jack Brabham and Roy Salvadori in Formula One. On the whole, they are unreliable but, at Monaco, Jack Brabham runs as high as third until encountering problems. It is a straw in the wind.

New rules in sports car racing preclude 'Manx Tails' running at Le Mans.

Jim Russell completes his hat-trick of British Formula Three Championships.

1958   Cooper formula cars have coil spring and double wishbone front suspension which also incorporates an anti-roll bar to enable the car to be fine-tuned to individual circuits.

Stirling Moss wins the Argentine Grand Prix in a Cooper entered by Rob Walker, then Maurice Trintignant wins the Monaco GP for Rob Walker and Cooper.

Coopers are also second (Salvadori) and third (Trintignant) in the German GP and Moss wins non-Championship races at Aintree and Caen.

Coopers clean up in Formula Two, winning all but three races. Winners for Cooper are: Maurice Trintignant (Pau and Charade), Stirling Moss (Goodwood), Tony Brooks (Aintree), Bruce McLaren (Silverstone, Brands Hatch and the Nürburgring), Ian Burgess (Crystal Palace and Snetterton), Stuart Lewis-Evans (Brands Hatch), Henry Taylor (Monthléry), Syd Jensen (Crystal Palace), Tim Parnell (Silverstone) and Jack Brabham (Brands Hatch and Casablanca).

1958 is the last year that Formula Three is an international category. Trevor Taylor wins the British Championship for Cooper and will go on to be a Lotus works driver.

1959   Jack Brabham wins the World Drivers' Championship and Cooper takes the Constructors' Cup.

Roy Salvadori leaves Cooper to join Aston Martin and Bruce McLaren replaces him while Masten Gregory has third car.

Cooper Formula cars all have upper wishbone at the rear.

Grands Prix are won by Brabham (Monaco, Holland, Britain); Moss (Portugal and Italy); and McLaren (United States). Moss wins non-Championship races at Goodwood and Oulton Park, and Brabham wins at Silverstone.

Every Formula Two race is won by Cooper: Jack Brabham (Goodwood and Brands Hatch), Jim Russell (Oulton Park and Silverstone), Mike Taylor (Aintree), Stirling Moss (Syracuse, Reims, Rouen and Clermont Ferrand), Jack Lewis (Monthléry), Tim Parnell (Silverstone and Mallory Park – twice), Maurice Trintignant (Pau), Roy Salvadori (Crystal Palace), Stan Hart (Edzell), Ron Carter (Silverstone), Chris Bristow (Aintree, Brands Hatch and Snetterton), Henry Taylor (Whitchurch), Tony Marsh (Zeltweg), Trevor Taylor (Rufforth) and Harry Schell (Monthléry).

Monaco (T48) sports racer introduced, and proves an immediate success.

Cooper experiments with Renault Dauphine fitted with Coventry Climax engine (T50) but cannot tame the suspension of the 'Rollover Renault'.

Cooper makes its last 500cc racing cars and Don Parker, a Cooper driver since 1955, takes his third British Championship.

First Formula Junior Cooper (T52) débuts at Boxing Day Brands Hatch meeting. On this occasion, it does not shine.

1960 Works run T53 'Lowline' cars from May onwards. The Lowline is the first Cooper with a straight tube spaceframe and also has coil springs and double wishbone suspension front and rear.

Jack Brabham and Cooper secure their respective Championships with five successive Grand Prix wins (Holland, Belgium, France, Britain and Portugal). McLaren, however, wins first race of the season (Argentina) in a T51 and is a clear second to Brabham in the World Drivers' Championship.

Brabham also wins non-Championship race at Oulton Park.

Cooper win most Formula Two races, but Ferrari and Porsche both have a much better start/win rate.

John Surtees makes his four-wheel début in a Cooper FJ at Goodwood, he is beaten only by Jim Clark (Lotus).

In Formula Junior, Cooper is second to Lotus in terms of wins in major events. Between them, the two British outfits send dozens of other makers to the wall.

1961 In common with other British constructors, Cooper has a thin time in the new 1500cc Formula One – the reason is that a new generation of engines is late in coming. Cooper runs slimmer version of the Lowline (T55) while customers may buy T53s.

Coventry Climax V8 engine first races at German GP in Brabham's Cooper, but Brabham spins on first lap.

Surtees wins non-Championship races at Snetterton and Goodwood and Brabham wins in Brussels and at Aintree.

Cooper's highest Championship finish is McLaren's third at Monza and Cooper drops to fourth in the Constructors' Cup.

Numerous ex-Formula Two Coopers run in Formula One – nine in the Italian GP, eleven in the Aintree 200. As well as Climax-powered cars, there are several with four-cylinder Maserati 150S units which prove to be uncompetitive, even in non-Championship races.

In the short-lived 3-litre Inter-Continental Formula, intended to be an alternative to F1, Cooper Lowlines win all five races.

Formula Two is dropped for 1961, so Formula Junior becomes the category immediately below F1. Much improved Cooper Mk II (T56) FJ cars, built like Lowlines in miniature, have very successful season.

Cooper goes to Indianapolis where Brabham shakes the establishment with modified F1 car (T54). Cooper sets in motion the 'rear engine revolution' at Indy, but fails to capitalise on its position.

Monaco sports racer continues to perform well in national events on both sides of the Atlantic, and Mk II version (T57) has coil spring rear suspension.

The Mini Cooper is launched in the summer of 1961 as an 'homologation special' to take advantage of the 1000cc class limit in racing and rallying. It will become a legend.

In the summer, the first MRD car, built for Formula Junior, appears. Motor Racing Developments is a new company established by Jack Brabham and Ron

Tauranac and the car is the first public indication that Brabham intends to go his own way. He leaves Cooper at the end of 1961.

1962   Bruce McLaren is joined by Tony Maggs in the Cooper F1 team running T60s which are T55s modified to accommodate the Climax V8 engine.

McLaren (T55) wins Lavant Cup at Goodwood for four-cylinder F1 cars and also Monaco GP (T60) and the non-Championship Reims GP (T60). These will be Cooper's only wins in the 1500cc Formula One. Maggs' (T60 is second in French GP.

McLaren is third in the Drivers' Championship with more points in total than Clark in second place, and Cooper is third behind BRM and Lotus in the Constructors' Cup.

The huge number of Coopers that had appeared in 1961 F1 races dwindle to the works cars and a handful of privateers.

Cooper has good year in Formula Junior, but clearly falls behind new cars from MRD, which are now called 'Brabhams'.

Monaco reaches Mk III version (T61)and American customers begin to experiment with home-grown V8 engines.

John Love wins the British Saloon Car Championship in a Mini Cooper run from the Cooper works.

Roy Salvadori's F2 Cooper-Climax T43 with young admirers at the 1957 Easter Monday Goodwood meeting. 'Salvo' was out of luck in the Lavant Cup which saw Brooks and Brabham score a Cooper 1–2.

1963   Cooper begins to decline in Formula One. Maggs is second in the French GP and McLaren is second in the Belgian GP and third at Monaco and Monza. McLaren is sixth in the drivers' championship and Cooper slips to fifth in the constructors' table. McLaren is also second in non-Championship races at Goodwood and Silverstone.

In Formula Junior, many customers opt for Ford-based engines, tuned by Cosworth and Holbay, while the works stay with BMC. Cooper's production of FJ cars declines and the Mk IV (T65) scores few successes. Cooper also experiments with BMC's 'Hydralastic' suspension, but does not proceed with it.

John Whitmore is second in the British Saloon Car Championship with a Cooper-run Mini Cooper.

Carroll Shelby buys Cooper Monacos and fits American V8 engines to create the 'King Cobra'. These are very successful in America and breed many imitators.

During the winter Owen Maddock, long-time Cooper draughtsman/designer leaves to freelance. His first project is a sports-racer for Bruce McLaren. Production models are made by Trojan and sold as 'McLaren-Elvas'.

1964   Former World Champion, Phil Hill, joins McLaren in the Formula One team. It is not a happy partnership, partly because the Cooper T73 is uncompetitive. McLaren is second in the Belgian and Italian Grands Prix, but these places are inherited rather than won. In other races, Cooper is usually out of the points.

Jackie Stewart and Warwick Banks, in Tyrrell-run Cooper T72s, have a splendid season in the new Formula Three, largely due to new short-stroke 970cc BMC engine which is also offered in an 'S' version of the Mini Cooper. BMC concentrates its efforts on the Tyrrell team and Cooper customer F3 cars enjoy little success.

Carroll Shelby's growing number of King Cobras goes from strength to strength in America, but Cooper makes no more sports cars after 1964. It is a missed opportunity because McLaren becomes more and more successful.

Warwick Banks wins European Touring Car Championship in 970cc Mini Cooper run by Ken Tyrrell.

A 1071cc Mini Cooper 'S' wins the Monte Carlo Rally driven by Paddy Hopkirk and Henry Liddon.

Cooper makes a twin-engined Mini with rallying in mind. John Cooper has very serious accident in the prototype when a component fails. John's lengthy convalescence has deleterious effect on the team.

In October, Charles Cooper dies of a heart attack. That, combined with his own injuries, causes John to sell Cooper Cars to the Chipstead Group, though he remains with the company.

The absence of Charles Cooper's hard-headed business acumen soon reflects on the prosperity of the outfit.

1965   Cooper is little more than a make-weight in Formula One despite employing Bruce McLaren and Jochen Rindt to drive the T77. The highlight of the year is the Belgian GP where Bruce is third.

The success of the Team Tyrrell F3 cars in 1964 leads to healthy orders for the lightly revised 1965 car, the T76. The optimism of the customers is misplaced, however, and the cars are not competitive. They win only three of the sixty-one important Formula Three races in 1965.

A similar model, the T75, is made for the new 1000cc Formula Two, but achieves no success.

The 1275cc Mini Cooper 'S' makes a huge impression in both racing and

Hugh Clifford's Cooper-Bristol in an Historic race at Brands Hatch in 1968. With the increased popularity of Historic racing, Cooper-Bristols have enjoyed a new lease of life and the best ones are usually to be seen at the sharp end of the field.

rallying. Timo Makinen wins the Monte Carlo Rally and Rally of 1000 Lakes.

John Rhodes joins Cooper's saloon car team and wins 1300cc class in the British Championship, as he will for the next three years. Warwick Banks in a 970cc version wins the 1000cc class and is runner-up in the series.

The performance of the Mini Coopers is the only bright spot for Cooper in 1965.

1966 Formula One becomes a 3-litre category and Cooper secures exclusive supply of Maserati V12 engines. It is a good move since some other teams are struggling to find an engine supply. The Maserati unit is installed in a new design (T81) which is Cooper's first monocoque chassis.

For the first time for some years, Cooper also makes F1 cars for privateers – these are driven by Jo Bonnier, Jo Siffert and Guy Ligier.

Initially, the works fields cars for Jochen Rindt and Richie Ginther, but Ginther is recalled by Honda in June and, at the same time, John Surtees leaves Ferrari and is snapped up by Cooper. The influence of Surtees develops the car and John is rewarded with a win in the Mexican GP and second in the German GP. Rindt is second in Belgium and the United States.

Surtees and Rindt are second and third in the Drivers' Championship and Cooper is third in the constructors' table albeit with more points (gross) than Ferrari in second.

Other Cooper single-seaters are made in tiny numbers and achieve no notable success – much of the reason is aerodynamic lift at the front of the car, but this is realised only later. BMC is no longer supplying engines and the works T83 Formula Three cars use Ford engines while the Cooper name continues to appear on Minis.

Mini Coopers take the first three places in the Monte Carlo Rally and are then disqualified over a technicality – victory goes instead to a French entry. The disqualification creates world-wide publicity for the Mini Cooper (which goes on to win five other international rallies in 1966) and sets the seal on the Mini Cooper legend.

In the British Saloon Car Championship, John Rhodes wins the 1300cc class again, but the title goes to John Fitzpatrick's Ford Anglia. The deciding factor is tyres since the Anglia, with its 13-inch wheels, can use rubber developed for Formula Three cars.

1967 John Surtees leaves for Honda and his replacement is Pedro Rodriguez who wins the first World Championship race of the year, the South African GP.

New designs from rivals appear while Cooper stands still. The cars are overweight and work on the engines to increase power merely makes the Maserati V12 unreliable. Apart from the win in South Africa, no Cooper finishes higher than fourth in a World Championship race. A 'lightweight' version (T81B) appears in late August, but it is too little, too late.

To all intents and purposes, Cooper has ceased to make customer single-seaters.

Mini Cooper becomes the first model to win seven major rallies in a single year, but 1967 is the last year that the car is capable of taking outright wins on a regular basis.

Works racing Minis receive fuel injection; John Rhodes wins the 1300cc class in the British Saloon Car Championship and is a close runner-up in the series.

1968 Direct sponsorship is permitted in Formula One, but Cooper is slow to latch on. The 1968 F1 car (T86B) is a development of the '67 car, and is powered by a V12 BRM engine originally developed for sports cars. The engine is neither powerful nor reliable and Cooper is in need of a new chassis (and designer).

Due to accidents, the Cooper F1 driver line-up changes frequently throughout the year, but no driver can make the car competitive. Lucien Bianchi is third at Monaco, but there are only five classified finishers and Bianchi finishes four laps down.

Mini Coopers are no longer serious candidates for outright wins in international rallies, but they continue to take class wins.

John Rhodes wins the 1300cc class in the British Saloon Car Championship and, in a private car, Gordon Spice wins the 1000cc class. In the European Touring Car Championship John Handley in a BMC-supported private car wins the 1000cc class and John Rhodes wins the 1600cc class in his 1300cc Cooper-run Mini. It is the Mini Cooper's swansong in international racing and is, perhaps, its finest hour.

1969 Cooper announces that it plans to make twenty-five cars for Formula 5000, but the project gets no further than a couple of prototypes which find no buyers.

A private Cooper T86B-Maserati runs in three F1 races and that is Cooper's only presence in international racing. The effects of the Cooper team are sold in the summer.

BMC takes over the running of works Mini Coopers, and John Handley and John Handley drive the cars. John Cooper puts together a private team, with backing from Britax, and runs Steve Neal and Gordon Spice.

The two teams race each other all season in the 1300cc class, provide furious racing, but take points from each other. The British Championship is won by Alec Poole in a private Mini Cooper running in the 1000cc class.

The Britax Mini Coopers are the last cars to be run from the Cooper works and the last team with which John Cooper is associated.

CHAPTER ONE

SMALL BEGINNINGS

Charles Cooper was a bit of a rough diamond – a good practical engineer with a short fuse and fixed ideas, but there was a good heart under the bluster. Charlie served in the First World War, was gassed and, fed up with hospital, discharged himself so he could get on with his life, while muttering about *bloody quacks*. Afterwards he rode in motorcycle trials, became mechanic/adviser to the racing driver and Land Speed Record contender, Kaye Don, and set up his own garage in Surbiton, Surrey.

The business prospered and Charlie started a small engineering works which subcontracted work from Hawker Aircraft. Just before the Second World War, he made caravans, which disassembled for easy storage over winter. Not many had been made when Cooper's small workshop was put over to war work.

During the war, plans were laid down by the Government of National Unity for a better world afterwards. While politicians devised reforms to health care and education, many motor racing enthusiasts dreamt of a rebirth of motor racing – racing for everyone. For many years, British motor racing had been dominated by Brooklands, a vast, concrete, banked track in Weybridge, Surrey. Donington Park, Leicestershire,

One of the earliest shots of a Cooper in action. Eric Brandon competes at the Luton Hoo hill climb in 1948 in one of the first two cars made. Note the wheels which are from a Fiat 500. Cooper's distinctive cast wheels appeared that year on the first batch of production cars.

opened in 1934, followed by Crystal Palace in 1937, but for many years Brooklands was the only circuit on the British mainland and therefore the appeal of motor racing was limited. Any sport that has only one venue will not reach the general public.

On the Continent, and in Ireland, racing went to the people because towns would close their streets once a year to hold a race. It was an annual festival and the tradition lives on in Monte Carlo and Pau. On mainland Britain, while Brooklands existed, it was an excuse not to permit racing on public roads so the sport grew around the track and was accessible only to those who lived near it. Among those were Charlie Cooper and his son, John. Charlie built an Austin Seven special for John's twelfth birthday. John recalls, 'I had nearly managed to complete a lap of Brooklands when I stopped by officials who gave me the bollocking of my life.'

For most people in Britain, however, motor racing remained inaccessible. Seaside resorts ran speed trials along the front – Brighton maintains the tradition to this day. Some, like Skegness in Lincolnshire and Southport in Lancashire, held races on their beaches. And there were hill climbs, trials, driving tests, treasure hunts and trails. A group of enthusiasts in the Bristol area, however, formed a group called CAPA, after the initials of the founders. CAPA encouraged racing around a field using home-made, low-cost specials – few, if any, cost more than £50.

During the war, correspondence in *Motor Sport*, combined with the example set by CAPA, generated the idea of a low-cost single-seater formula. The rules were simple: cars had to be of no more than 500cc and no less than 500lb. No more than 1 gallon of fuel

John Cooper won the second heat at the 1950 British GP meeting and was sixth in the final with his father Charles, twelfth.

Another driver in the very important Formula Three race which supported the 1950 British GP, the first-ever World Championship race, was Eric Brandon. Eric has a boyhood friend of John Cooper and the owner of one of the first two Coopers built.

could be carried and the rules advised that 'a body is desirable'. The capacity limit suggested a motorcycle engine and that is what almost everyone used. John Cooper himself once said, famously, that the key to the formula was a 'four-wheeled motorcycle'.

The idea hit the right button and the Vintage Sports Car Club (VSCC) agreed to include the 500cc class in its events. Members of CAPA addressed groups of enthusiasts up and down the land and, to launch the new movement, they formed the Iota project. Iota could supply components, or even a complete kit, to help anyone who wanted to join in the fun. For anyone who did so, in the immediate postwar period, it was an act of faith. France had held a race meeting on the streets of Paris within four weeks of VJ Day, but Britain had nothing except hope. Its three pre-war circuits were out of commission, and how do you have motor racing without a single circuit? Petrol rationing restricted the private motorist to perhaps 30 miles a week and basic items such as clothes, and most food, were rationed.

Despite the unpromising circumstances, Charlie and John Cooper decided to build a car for the new class. Actually, it would be two cars because John's boyhood friend, Eric Brandon, came on board. They scoured scrapyards for wrecked Fiat 500 Topolini. In essence they took the front suspension from two Fiats, separated them by a box-section ladder frame, added telescopic dampers, popped in a JAP Speedway engine, made by J.A. Prestwick, behind the driver, and clothed the result with a simple aluminium body. Actually, Charlie and John had the idea, but most of the work was carried out by Michael 'Ginger' Devlin who had joined Cooper at the end of the war on a wage of 18s (90p) a week. Years later it would be Ginger who would build the first Mini Cooper and run the fabulously successful works Mini racing

One of the earliest production Coopers, competing in a hillclimb.

team. Ginger recalls, 'Charlie would sack me every week or so, just for form's sake, but John would always take me back.' Whereas the Old Man was a crusty old devil, John was softer. He was, is, a man with warmth, a sense of humour, and a gift for friendship. To a certain extent, he and Charlie acted 'Good Cop, Bad Cop' but it was entirely subconscious. It was just the way the two men were.

From his father, John inherited a love for cars and motor racing. Like his father he was also a fine intuitive engineer, a man with no great formal education, but one who possessed a good eye for what would work. The pragmatic approach of the Coopers, father and son, would lay the foundation of the success of Cooper Cars. Most subsequent Coopers were developed from the original – a car invented rather than designed. In other words, this important succession of cars was created along the lines, 'Why don't we do this?' 'Will it work?' 'It could work, if we did that.'

Charlie and John chose the mid-engined configuration because they reckoned that the most effective method to transfer power was by a short chain to the rear wheels. It sounds obvious, but other people tried putting the engine in front of the driver, because that's where almost every car had its engine and, apart from the few who adopted front-wheel drive, they suffered the friction loss and mechanical complications of chains perhaps 15 or 16 feet long. The Coopers got the formula right at a time when all sorts of strange ideas were in the air. Some claimed that light cars could not hold the road because weight was needed to keep them on the ground. Others said that a car's body made little or no difference to its performance.

Charlie and John Cooper went for simplicity, but they did everything right in detail. Components were properly made – a residue from the work Charlie had done for Hawker Aircraft. There were still a few things to learn about engine installation, however, as John discovered when subsidiary parts broke when power was applied. But a new engine mounting solved the problem.

The first Cooper ran in 1946, but only in hill climbs. Britain's only 1946 race meeting, held on an ex-RAF airfield, did not have a 500cc race because there weren't enough cars to make a grid. A year later there were sixteen 500cc cars in more or less ready condition and a race was announced at Brough airfield, near Hull, as part of a motorcycle meeting. Four cars were entered, but none arrived and the reasons included 'no transport' and 'unable to arrange leave'. Things were tight in Britain in the Austerity period.

John Cooper and Eric Brandon, therefore, ran only in sprints and hill climbs, where they were often beaten by the New Zealander, Colin Strang. Strang had taken a standard Fiat 500 chassis, with its quarter-elliptic spring rear suspension, and had installed a Vincent-HRD engine amidships. In those early postwar events, Strang had the advantage mainly due to the power of his engine.

At Britain's second postwar meeting, at Gransden Lodge in 1947, there was a 500cc race. Strang was the fastest man on the track, but Eric Brandon won the race. A Cooper, therefore, won the first race it ran in.

Then the Coopers decided to put their car into production. It sounds a simple thing to do, but 1947 was not the best year to start a new industry. The year began with one of the worst winters in history; the entire country was under snow roads and railways were closed. Coal could not get through to power stations so power cuts

This elderly Cooper Mk IV was still giving service to J. Denty in hill climbs in 1966, more than sixteen years after it was made.

Stirling Moss, then aged twenty, in his Cooper-JAP at the 1950 British Grand Prix Meeting. Note the lucky horseshoe – Stirling partly financed Cooper through money won show jumping. As a lucky

mascot, the horseshoe was less than satisfactory because Stirling was leading the final of the 500cc when, at the last corner, the piston in his engine broke and he had to be content with second.

This Mk IV was first used by Peter Collins, who starred for Ferrari in the late 1950s. Twenty years after its construction it was still running in hill climbs, stripped to save weight. Note the tiny fuel tank – you only need a thimbleful of fuel on most British hills.

were frequent and Buckingham Palace set an example to the nation by being lit with candles. Then there was the matter of paying America the debts accumulated during the war. Rations were shorter than during the worst days of hostilities – even bread supplies were restricted. Worse was to come: on 1 December 1947, the basic petrol ration was withdrawn altogether. Unless you had a special reason – you were a vet or a physician, perhaps – you had no petrol. That is why the British motor racing calendar was pretty thin in early 1948.

When the Coopers put their 500 car into production, they faced a few problems. John Cooper recalls:

Raw materials were restricted by the government, but I bought a stack of Morrison shelters, which were basically steel tables under which a family could shelter in the event of an air raid. The tops of the shelters were made from high quality steel, and we used these to make the suspension castles. The legs of the shelters became the jigs and we were still using them to make jigs right to the end of making cars.

Wheels were a problem; you just couldn't get them, so we cast our own. The scrapyards were bursting with ex-military kit made from aluminium, including aluminium sheeting which had been intended make or mend aircraft. We cast our wheels from that until we could get magnesium alloy.

We found a marine scrapyard who could supply us with cylinder liners of scrap marine diesel engines. We sawed 'em up, cutting them like you'd slice a Swiss roll. These were our brake drums and we cast them into the centre of our wheels.

James Burgoyne, an enthusiastic amateur, is lapped by Stuart Lewis-Evans (car no. 1) at Silverstone in 1953. Lewis-Evans would go on to drive for Connaught, Ferrari, Aston Martin and Vanwall. The world lost an outstanding talent when Stuart was mortally injured in 1958.

Seven cars were completed in early 1948 at a price of £575 each. The most significant customer was the eighteen-year-old Stirling Moss, who ten years on would give Cooper its first World Championship win. At the time, the basic petrol ration was still suspended, so British motor racing consisted of just a single hill climb, at Prescott, until the meagre ration was restored on 1 June.

The first motor races of 1948 took place at the Brough airfield. They were for 500cc cars and were slotted into a motorcycle meeting. At Brough, there were three heats and a final for the cars, and a further handicap. Stirling Moss and Stan Coldham each won a heat in their Coopers, while the third heat was won by Don Truman in a Marwyn. Marwyn was a Welsh outfit also building cars for sale, but Truman's win in a heat at Brough was the only success it ever had. Stirling won the final and also the handicap. He then won the 500cc race at Goodwood in September and was ten seconds *a lap* ahead of the field in the Silverstone race in October, but he had to retire. The race was won by Irwin 'Spike' Rhiando in a Cooper, however, while John Cooper was second, Sir Francis Samuelson was third and Eric Brandon was fourth, all in Coopers. Cooper had arrived.

Cooper had also made its first sports cars. The T4 was based on the 500 design. It had a 650cc Triumph Twin engine behind the driver and was clothed in a pretty streamlined body, but it was unreliable and slow. A better option was the half dozen or so front-engined cars laid out on the 500 chassis. They tended to have MG engines, but others were used, and buyers not only sorted out the power units, they also sorted out the bodywork and most chose slipper bodies with cycle mudguards.

Bill Whitehouse was a long-time Cooper exponent, eventually racing a private 1500cc F2 car with some success. At the 1950 British GP meeting he was a close second to Moss in the first heat of the Formula Three event, but his Mk III Cooper-Norton retired in the final.

Jim Russell racing a Cooper in 1952. Jim would take a hat-trick of wins in the Formula Three championship, 1955–7. He raced a Cooper Monaco and an F2 Cooper with success and seemed destined for Formula One before a serious accident curtailed his career. The Jim Russell Racing Schools are now world famous.

In the right hands, and with the right engine, the Coopers were competitive in British club events for many years.

In 1949, things were improving as far as motor racing was concerned: Silverstone was in regular use, Goodwood (West Sussex) ran three meetings and races were run at Lulsgate (now Bristol Airport), Blandford (Dorset), Gamston (Nottinghamshire), Croft (Co. Durham), Winfield (Scotland) and Castle Combe (Wiltshire). All ran races for 500cc cars, or 'Midgets' as some sections of the national press called them.

THE BIRTH OF FORMULA THREE

The success of 500cc racing in Britain caused people abroad to take interest and soon cars were being built in many countries. Then the FIA, the sport's governing body, announced that the 500cc formula would become the International Formula Three from 1950. It was the first time that the sport had a Formula Three, and it was the first International class of racing to originate in Britain. At the time, Cooper ruled the roost. Few of the cars built with Iota components amounted to much. The Marwyn project had folded, deservedly, and had been taken over by Cyril Kieft. There were some successful home-built specials in Britain, but Continental builders were confident of success.

Britain had been a second-rate nation in motor racing at international level. Sure, it had come up with a new racing formula, but what did that prove? Continental makers were convinced they'd soon take over.

The rules for the new International formula were little changed from the original concept – minimum weight dropped from 500lb to 440lb and a minimum ground clearance of 4 inches was imposed.

The Swedes usually ran their cars on speedway tracks, while the Germans frequently used autobahns, and so they often used streamlined bodies. The Italians were expected to dominate since they made some sophisticated multi-cylinder 500cc engines but, in the event, they flopped. To be successful in Formula Three an engine needed torque and almost every race would be won by either a JAP or Norton single-cylinder unit.

By the end of 1950, nobody from the Continent had displaced Cooper from its position at the top of the tree. The Italians sulked and turned to their own version of Formula Three – a national 750cc category where the cars were almost all front-engined and the engines were mainly based on Fiat units.

It was in 1949 that some owners began to fit 998cc V-twin JAP engines to their Coopers so they could run in Formula Two and Formula Libre events; quite often they would swap engines during a meeting to run in two races. In 1950, Harry Schell entered such a car in the Monaco Grand Prix, which made this Cooper's first appearance in a World Championship race. Schell was last in practice and was out on the first lap after being caught up in a multiple shunt. Eight years later, a Cooper would win the Monaco Grand Prix, fair and square.

Supporting the Monaco Grand Prix was a race for Formula Three cars. It would not be until 1959 that such a support race would be run again, but the first was won by Stirling Moss from Schell, both in Coopers, with Don Parker third in his Parker-CFS, one of the few specials that was still competitive by 1950.

Cooper now dominated Formula Three. A number of outfits rose to challenge it, however. Cyril Kieft had taken over the Marwyn project and produced a revised car

Peter Collins, who would become one of the world's greatest drivers, began his racing career with a Cooper. In the support race at the 1950 British GP meeting, his Norton-powered car finished third in the final, just 2.4 seconds behind the winner and 0.2 second off Stirling Moss in second.

under his own name. It wasn't very successful save in hill climbs. Meanwhile, Paul Emery's Emerysons were front-engined and had front-wheel drive. Styled after a Mercedes-Benz W163 Grand Prix car, they had their moments of success. From a driver's point of view, the fact that an Emeryson was different to the Coopers, and Cooper-copies, which dominated every field, meant they could perhaps negotiate better starting money from race organisers on the Continent.

One of the things that Formula Three brought was the chance for British drivers to race on the Continent and it was common for perhaps twenty to be on the grid of a race if it was not too far from the Channel ports. The running costs for a Formula Three car were low and, with starting money, prize money and trade bonuses, successful drivers could make a decent living from their racing.

This was not what the founders of the 500cc movement had in mind when they proposed their formula. By 1950, the category had become professional and the day when the home-builder could arrive with a special and hope to get among the prizes had already gone save for one or two cases. JAP engines still ruled, but the 'double-knocker' Norton engine would soon arrive and when it did, Formula Three would not merely be dominated by Norton engines, but by Norton engines prepared by certain tuners, notably Francis Beart and Steve Lancefield. Having engines specially tuned raised drivers' budgets and, because Beart and Lancefield could deal with just a limited number of engines, only those lucky enough to be on their customer lists stood a realistic chance of winning important races. In order to get his hands on one of the new 'double-knocker' Norton engines, Les Leston bought a new Norton motorcycle, removed the engine and sold on the rest of the bike. Les would be the British Formula Three Champion in 1954, driving a Cooper.

It was also in 1950 that a former motorcycle grass track, Brands Hatch, was given a tarmac surface. It did not then have the loop to Druids, cars ran anti-clockwise and races had a rolling start behind a pace vehicle. Though just a mile to the lap, Brands Hatch, Kent, was ideal for Formula Three cars and the Half Litre Club began to run meetings devoted to 500cc cars. Including heats, there could be eleven or twelve races on the card, with 'Junior' and 'Senior' events and races for the home-builder.

At the *Daily Telegraph* Trophy meeting at Brand Hatch in October 1950, there was a total of forty-five entries and thirty-two of them were Coopers. Cooper had became the first British company ever to build single-seaters in quantity and more than 400 Formula Three cars would be made, all of them developments of the original special. Multi-tubular frames would appear and disc brakes would be used, but the suspension and basic layout would remain unchanged and it would be enough to see off most of the opposition, most of the time, for ten years. And it was all done by Charlie and John assessing any promising new car on the scene and saying, 'They're doing that, why don't we do this?'

CHAPTER TWO

GRAND PRIX RACERS

During 1951, Eric Brandon and Alan Brown ran Cooper-Nortons under the banner of Ecurie Richmond. Alan recalls the season: 'I found a patron in Jimmy Richmond who, being 22 stone, couldn't fit into a racing car, and Jimmy provided the transporter. Because Eric and I had been reasonably successful by ourselves, running together as a team, we also secured a number of trade supporters, fuel companies, spark plugs and so on.' By horse trading, they also secured a supply of double-knocker Norton engines and, equally crucial, links to the leading tuners.

Ecurie Richmond presented a professional face and it found all manner of responses from the opposition. Alan says, 'Some people hated us because they thought that we were trying too hard, but race organisers loved us. I was very keen on professional presentation and had my overalls made in pale blue with a distinctive cross-over zip across the front. That sort of attention to detail didn't cost much, but it's how we wanted to go racing.'

Brown and Brandon had a terrific season. They seemed to rise to the big occasion and Ecurie Richmond was unquestionably the team of the year in Formula Three. Thus Alan won the Luxembourg Grand Prix and, in the very next race, a support event at the International Trophy, it was Brandon first and Brown second. Alan

Les Leston (Cooper, no. 70) passes the Kieft of Charles Headland at Silverstone in September 1952. Leston went on to win with Headland third.

Francis Beart was one of the two best tuners of the Norton double-knocker engine and he also modified and entered Coopers. He is seen working on Colin Davis's car at the 1956 British Grand Prix meeting. Note the spare wheel with wire spokes and an Al-fin brake drum.

Ken Wharton's Mk II Cooper-Bristol in the paddock at Goodwood. The triple downdraught Solex carburettors made the engine very tall; hence the high bonnet line.

Mike Hawthorn made his name with a Cooper-Bristol and his performances in 1952 led directly to a contract with the Ferrari. He is seen here at Silverstone in 1958 when he brought his Dino 246 home second to team-mate and close pal, Peter Collins. By the end of the year, Collins was dead and Mike was the first British World Champion.

recalls: 'We would often take it in turns to win, which is why Eric won one of the British Formula Three Championships and I won another.

'We became a big attraction and could demand good starting money. It was between £100 and £200 in Britain but perhaps £1,000 each on the Continent – and that was more than a car cost. On top of that we had trade money, prize money and bonus money, so we made a very good living, but we worked at it. As soon as we came back from a trip to Europe, my engine would go to Francis Beart, Eric's would go to Steve Lancefield, and we had spare engines ready to bolt in. We finished up with four engines apiece, which was unheard of at the time. It seemed to me that there was a right way, and a wrong way, of doing things, and we were doing things properly.' This was definitely not what the founding fathers of the 500 movement had in mind, but then the movement had grown from the original enthusiasts racing round a field. Nobody then had dreamed that countries would be running races they'd call a 'Grand Prix', or that drivers would make a living from 500 racing.

Stirling Moss had been the first driver to adopt a professional attitude in 500 racing; by the end of 1951 he had enjoyed two years racing on the Continent with HWM in Formula Two, and had signed as the Jaguar works team leader. The 500 movement bred drivers like Moss, the Ecurie Richmond team and people like Don Parker and Les Leston at one end and, at the other, the guy with a home-made special and a mate to help him.

During the 1951 Luxembourg Grand Prix, which Alan won, the promising driver, Alf Bottoms, was killed. Bottoms, a former Speedway rider, had developed a very promising design, the JBS, which had caused Cooper some problems during the 1950

Five days after Mike Hawthorn became an overnight star at the 1952 Easter Monday Goodwood meeting, he was in action with his Cooper-Bristol at Ibsley. Mike took two wins. After his first five races with the car, Mike's tally was four wins and one second – and the second was behind a 4.5-litre Formula One Ferrari.

season. Alf had put the car into production and it was bought by some leading drivers, and won races, but after Alf was killed the project petered-out. Who knows how motor racing history might have changed had Alf Bottoms lived to realise his potential.

A more sustained challenge came from Cyril Kieft. Cyril had been in his early twenties when he managed one of the largest steel mills in Europe but, when the British steel industry was nationalised in 1948, he left. Supported by a foundry business of his own, he looked for a challenge for his energy and found it in motor racing. In late 1950, Kieft was approached by Ken Gregory, Stirling Moss's manager, to take over a 500cc project. Conceived by Dean Delamont, John A. Cooper (Technical Editor of *The Autocar*) and Ray Martin, it was intended for Moss. £120 exchanged hands and Kieft found himself in possession of an advanced design with all-independent suspension by rubber bands. He also found himself with a direct line to Moss who became a director of Kieft Cars. In the hands of Stirling Moss the prototype Kieft was virtually unbeatable, but it was destroyed in an accident and Moss discovered that the replacement, production-Kieft was poorly made and felt like a different car. Early in 1952 Moss resigned as a director Kieft Cars and switched to a Cooper.

Kieft also entered a works car for Don Parker, a man who had turned forty before he'd even seen a racing car. Parker, who had developed his own Parker-CFS to a high level of competitiveness, now proceeded to do the same to the Kieft. Kieft provided the components and Don modified them – they were really Parker-Kieft Specials. And they used Lancefield-tuned Norton engines. Don was built like a jockey, he never

Mike Hawthorn's Cooper-Bristol is unloaded at Ibsley. The Hawthorn équipe had yet to get round to painting the car. It was dark green by the time Mike made his World Championship début at the Belgian GP. There he qualified sixth from twenty-two starters and finished an incredible fourth, beaten only by works cars.

Stirling Moss at Goodwood in the 1953 Lavant Cup in the hapless Cooper-Alta. Like the Kieft F3 car which Moss drove, this was designed by John A. Cooper, Technical Editor of *The Autocar*, but Cooper Cars supplied some parts. The car was an unmitigated disaster.

Alan Brown in the one-off Cooper-Alfa Romeo at Goodwood in 1953. Bernie Rodger, a mechanic with pretensions to be an engineer, fitted a de Dion rear axle. Once when Duncan Hamilton drove the car at Goodwood, he made a racing start and the back axle fell off. That sort of thing did not happen to standard Coopers, which probably had fewer breakages than any other make.

Another shot of the Cooper-Alfa Romeo, in the paddock at Goodwood.

weighed more than 8 stone in his life, but he used to drill every possible component to save weight and even drove without socks or underwear so as not to carry the extra ounce or two.

When the Brits set their minds to motor racing, they flattened the opposition and it was not only the Italians who had begun to lose interest in Formula Three by the end of 1951. For the first time in motor racing history, the British had the best cars, best engines, best tuners and the most determined drivers. It was a turning point.

Parker became Cooper's main opposition from mid-1951 to the end of 1954. It was in that period that Parker achieved the majority of his 126 wins in Formula Three. He won the main British Championship in 1952 and 1953, and was denied his hat-trick by half a point in 1954. Don Parker was the fly in Cooper's ointment, but his cars were special, as was the man himself. It was Cooper who continued to make the best series-produced cars.

The threat from Kieft caused Cooper to redesign their Formula Three cars for 1952. The overall layout remained as before, but the chassis was completely tubular whereas previously it had box-section lower rails. It now had four main tubes, the upper tubes braced by drilled channel pieces and it was 25lb lighter than the car it replaced.

During 1951, the Coopers built a streamlined 500cc car for one of their customers, Bill Aston, to tackle some international speed records on the banked track at Monthléry on the outskirts of Paris. It was also raced by, among others,

Cooper's first sports cars were based on the 500cc chassis but with the engine in the front. Customers chose their engine and body and Jack Sears, a future British Saloon Car champion, chose an MG unit and this slipper body. . . .

. . . The car's next owner did not agree with Jack's choice so LLV 1 was fitted with what appears to be a Microplas Sirocco fibreglass body. It is seen at the Great Auclum hill climb in 1955 in the hands of R.D. Jennings.

Believe it or not, beneath this copy of the Alfa Romeo Disco Volante (flying saucer) body there lurks a Cooper Formula Three chassis. John Riseley-Pritchard fitted Connaught-modified Lea-Francis engine at the front and the car showed some promise until it was written off by a mechanic in a road accident.

John Cooper, who still enjoyed the odd event when pressure of business would allow.

For several years there was end-of-season rivalry between makers of 500cc cars. Kieft and Arnott both went record breaking at Monthléry, and Daphne Arnott recalls the 1953 record season. She and her team were preparing their own streamliner when Cooper got to Monthléry a few days earlier and established a batch of records. Daphne was one of the first to congratulate her rivals and she sent off a telegram: 'What was the matter? Was the handbrake jammed?' John responded: 'Many thanks for message. Diagnosis incorrect. Handbrake okay. Gear lever jammed. Records taken in bottom.' The Arnott team then went on to have a very successful record session. It almost goes without saying that the first people to wire congratulations to Daphne were John and Charlie Cooper.

Bill Aston's 1951 streamliner was later bought by the American, Pete Lovely, who fitted it with a 1.5-litre VW-derived Porsche engine to make the 'Pooper'. It sounds like something only a very brave, or foolish, person would do since the chassis had been designed for a 500cc engine, but Lovely had considerable success with his car. At different times the Pooper was run as a single-seater with open wheels and as centre-seat sports car (with a side seat for a midget). In 1955 the Pooper won the SCCA's Class F Modified national championship.

The chassis of Cooper Formula Three cars were put to all sorts of uses. Mike Cannon, a trials specialist, made a pretty front-engined coupé with an Austin A30 engine. John Riseley-Prichard had a Connaught-powered car fitted with a fair copy

Many Mk I Cooper-Bristols were converted to sports cars in 1953. This is actually the ex-Hawthorn car and it still exists in this form. First driven by Alan Brown, with great success, by late 1954 it was in the hands of Tom Kyffin. The few spectators seem more concerned with their soggy lot at Davidstow, a former airfield which remains Cornwall's only motor racing circuit, than with the action.

of the original Alfa Romeo Disco Volante body, and it was a very rapid motor car for a very short time – until a mechanic wrote it off on the road.

Alan Brown says: 'We made enough money from our Formula Three racing in 1951 to think of expanding and, for 1952, we decided to supplement the Formula Three cars with a couple of Formula Two Cooper-Bristols. We were the official Cooper works team, but when it came to building the cars, we had to arrange a lot of the work ourselves.' The Cooper-Bristol was more or less a Formula Three car on steroids, but with the engine in the front. It had a similar box-section chassis frame and suspension and the driver sat high in the airstream because he was on top of the prop shaft. (The elimination of that would be one of the advantages of Cooper's later mid-engined layout.)

The six-cylinder Bristol engine had been obtained from Germany as part of war reparations – originally it had been the unit designed for the BMW 328 sports car. It was, however, made by the Bristol Car Company who made some changes. As well as powering Bristol sports saloons, specially tuned versions were supplied to AFN Ltd for their Frazer Nash sports cars. It was a tall engine so the Cooper-Bristol, with its high ground clearance, always looked slightly ungainly.

Bill Aston had permission to copy the chassis for his Aston-Butterworth Formula Two project. In his two cars, Aston used flat-four air-cooled AJB engines designed by Archie Butterworth. It was a promising project save for the fact that the engine, unless it was tuned to the *nth* degree, had a tendency to catch fire. A mere detail.

John Cooper in one of the streamlined record cars on the banking at the Avus track in Berlin. The overall line of the T39 'Manx Tail' sports car is evident in the streamliner's body. Below John is a German Formula Three car, a BMW-engined Monopoletto, which is being lapped. The designer of the Monopoletto, Helmut Polensky, ignored John's dictum, which was to make a four-wheeled motorcycle, and his cars were outclassed from the start.

ENTER MIKE HAWTHORN

Early in 1952 the French authorities had announced that all their major single-seater races would be for the 2-litre Formula Two. Alfa Romeo had withdrawn from racing, BRM could not get its cars to the starting line, so that left just Ferrari plus a sprinkling of obsolete cars. Other race organisers followed the French so the FIA decided to run the World Championship to Formula Two in 1952/3 and introduce a 2½-litre Formula One in 1954. Overnight the Cooper-Bristol became a World Championship contender.

Alan Brown continues, 'Eric [Brandon], who lived near the Cooper works, made sure we that got all the best bits, while what was left over went on the third car which was being made for youngster called Mike Hawthorn. We got our cars late, but were able to give them a shake-down on Odiam airfield. Eric didn't think that Mike would give us any trouble, we were the reigning Formula Three champs, after all, but I had watched Mike carefully and wasn't so sure.'

John Michael Hawthorn was born in April 1929, in Mexborough, Yorkshire, but when he was three the family moved to Farnham, Surrey. His father, Leslie, was an engineer and the move was motivated by a desire to be near Brooklands because Leslie's passion was motorcycles and tuning them. With a friend, he opened the Tourist Trophy Garage, which sold and tuned motorcycles and cars. The garage prospered and Leslie made a name for himself among the Brooklands crowd as a

Lionel Leonard originally had this Cooper-MG (JOY 500) bodied in the style of a Ferrari *Barchetta*. Leonard sold it to Cliff Davis (pictured) who had a similar body made for his 1953 Tojeiro-Bristol (LOY 500). Davis's Tojeiro became the inspiration for the AC Ace and, hence, the Cobra, but JOY 500 is the distant ancestor.

Another shot of JOY 500, this time at a club meeting at Silverstone in late 1954 in the hands of its new owner, P. Jackson. A Cooper-MG owned by Brian Lister had been more than a casual inspiration to John Tojeiro (he'd passed a tape measure over it) and when Charlie Cooper saw a Tojeiro chassis on the AC stand at the 1953 London Motor Show he was heard to exclaim, "Ere, that's our car.'

More early Cooper sports cars used this style of slipper body than any other. This is A. Hitchings in an MG-powered example enjoying a club race at Silverstone in October 1952.

tuner and racer. Being brought up in such an atmosphere, with regular trips to the nearby circuit, fostered a love of motor racing in Mike. He went away to boarding school where he was good at games, and was popular, but he was not interested in school work, only in motorcycles and, as he grew older, in drinking and in girls – just like his father.

When Mike left school, he pursued speed, beer and girls with zest, and occasionally competed in motorcycle trials. Then there were trips to Goodwood to watch motor racing and, as his passion for the sport grew, so his father decided to indulge his only son and bought him an 1100cc Riley Ulster Imp. Hawthorn made quite a mark and won the *Motor Sport* Brooklands Memorial Trophy, which was virtually the Championship of Goodwood. People took notice of the tall, good-looking youngster – one of them was Bob Chase.

Chase was a friend of Leslie's and when he heard that Cooper was to build a Bristol-engined Formula Two car, he picked up a telephone and ordered one for Mike. There was a bit of a snag because it had been proposed to build the first three cars to be run under the banner Ecurie Richmond, with the third car to be handled by John Cooper. John had raced against Hawthorn in one of his own Cooper sports cars and had been very impressed, so he sportingly let Mike have the car destined for himself. Leslie gathered together a team of first-class mechanics who had to battle against a tight deadline since both chassis and engine were

Ken Flint's Cooper-MG had this inelegant – and probably inefficient – body in 1953.

delivered late. When the car arrived at Goodwood for the Easter Monday meeting it was still unpainted.

It was the first time that Mike had driven a single-seater, or a car as powerful, and it was only as he sat in pole position for the Lavant Cup for Formula Two cars that he realised he'd never made a racing start in the car. He remembered something he'd read about how top drivers did it; and it worked. Mike led from the line to the chequered flag and set fastest lap along the way. Then he did the same in the Formula Libre Chichester Cup – and down in fifth place, driving a Cooper-Bristol, was Juan-Manuel Fangio. Next, in the Richmond Trophy for Formula One cars, Mike was beaten only by Froilan González driving the 'Thin Wall Special', which was actually a 4½-litre Ferrari 375. Hawthorn slotted into second place at the start and stayed there until the end.

Next morning the papers were full of the new British motor racing star. In a single day he had arrived and he decided that from then on he was a racing driver. He left the Chelsea College of Engineering, where he'd been studying on a sandwich course, but came away from it with his trademark – a bow tie. One of the lecturers had worn one and he'd been a bit of a martinet who had bawled Mike out for arriving late. Mike's response had been to start wearing a bow tie, and to continue to arrive late.

A cool look down the entry lists for the races at Goodwood finds them a little short on quality, and the Formula Two race was only a six-lapper which lasted

A rare shot of Thruxton in August, 1952. The Hampshire airfield circuit took over from Goodwood as the home of the British Automobile Racing Club in 1968, but conditions were still primitive as the Formula Three field starts the final of their event. John Coombs (Cooper, no. 96) won and set fastest lap. He would later become a leading motor racing entrant.

Car no. 89 is the Cooper of Austen Nurse and no. 93 is David Boshier-Jones's Kieft. Boshier-Jones would find fame in hill climbing, usually driving a Cooper. Farthest away is Ivor Bueb driving an Iota (no. 92). 'Ivor the Driver' would go on to drive in Formula One and be a double-winner at Le Mans.

barely ten minutes. To be hard-nosed about it, Hawthorn really had only the two other Coopers to beat – Fangio had been hired by the organisers and had been shoe-horned into a car at the last minute. It was an experience he preferred to forget. Further, Mike had certain advantages. For one thing his father was a brilliant engine tuner but, more to the point, Leslie Hawthorn had brewed a special fuel containing nitromethane imported from America. This was perfectly legal, few formula cars ran on petrol, but nitromethane was special and the entire team was sworn to secrecy.

Five days after Goodwood Hawthorn was in action again, and won two races at Ibsley. The opposition wasn't much, but it kept his name in the headlines. His first real test was in the International Trophy at Silverstone a few weeks later. It had as good a field as could be gathered at the time, lacking only the works Ferraris. Hawthorn won his heat and was battling for the lead in the final when his gear-lever worked loose. The Goodwood performance was no fluke.

Mike was making a name for himself, yet Cooper's contribution was considerable. In Britain alone it had opposition from Frazer Nash, Connaught, Aston-Butterworth, Alta, HWM and ERA. The ERA was also Bristol-engined and it had Stirling Moss as its driver, yet Stirling wasted a season by driving it. The Coopers with their pragmatic approach had produced a race winner while ERA, with much greater resources, wasn't competitive even with Moss at the wheel.

Charlie and John had been joined on the design side by Owen Maddock, a draughtsman who also played Souzaphone with some well-known jazz bands, including the Mick Mulligan Band when George Melly was the vocalist. Owen made more money in the evenings than ever Charlie Cooper ever paid him. A legend has grown, from various sources including George Melly, that Owen seduced girls by playing them Sidney Bechet records. Owen says, 'I was still living with my parents and when I had girls in my room and wanted to drown the sound of us making love, I'd play Sidney Bechet because his records lasted longer than anyone else!' Another legend is that Cooper drawings were chalk marks on the garage floor, but Owen drew proper blueprints – and he still has many of them. Owen, a slightly off-beat man, gradually had more and more input into the design of the cars.

The Cooper-Bristol's World Championship début came in the Swiss Grand Prix. Alan Brown finished fifth to score Cooper's first Championship points. Mike Hawthorn made his World Championship début in the Belgian Grand Prix where he finished a fine fourth, with Alan Brown sixth.

Brown and Brandon were out of their depth at World Championship level, but Hawthorn was third in the British GP – where seven Cooper-Bristols started – and fourth in the Dutch. The highlight of his year, however, was third place in a Formula Libre race at Boreham. It had promised to be little more than an interesting national event, but there were two V16 BRMs present and three 4½-litre Ferraris, so Hawthorn had no right to finish higher than sixth, but it rained. It didn't just rain, it bucketed down and, one by one, Hawthorn passed the larger cars until, after forty-two laps, he had a 40 second lead. Then the rain stopped and Luigi Villoresi's Ferrari hauled him in. Mike would still have taken second but his flywheel began to work loose and one of the other Ferraris overtook him.

This Cooper sports car, driven by E.A. Jauney at Silverstone in 1954, was fitted with a Rover engine and someone's idea of styling. Both choices were bizarre.

Horace Gould's Cooper-MG at Silverstone in 1953. Gould, usually called 'burly Bristolian', went on to achieve some fame as an F1 privateer with a Maserati 250F.

In mid-November Mike received an invitation from Enzo Ferrari to visit him and, soon afterwards, it was announced that he was to join Ferrari for 1953. Cooper had provided Hawthorn with the ladder which would take him ever onwards, ever upwards, towards being the 1958 World Champion.

A Mk II Formula Two car followed for Cooper in 1953. The main difference was a sleeker body without the characteristic bonnet scoop of the original. Owen Maddock had split the radiator core and spread the two halves so that cool air could pass between them to the carburettors. About fourteen Mk IIs would be made and fitted with Bristol, Alta, and Alfa Romeo engines, but the Mk II proved disappointing largely because the opposition had made much greater strides in terms of power. The venerable Bristol and Alta engines were no match for the increasing number of Ferrari and Maserati Formula Two cars in private hands.

Alan Brown did a few races and his sixth place in the German Grand Prix was Cooper's best World Championship result, but in 1953 sixth place did not score points. Coopers took third, fourth and fifth in the Syracuse Grand Prix but only after all the Ferraris had retired. They won a few minor British races, but were more likely to be beaten by Connaught.

Some Cooper Formula Two cars were converted to sports cars, with a variety of body styles. Most of these have since been restored to original specification for

The first four Cooper-Bristols line up at Goodwood on Easter Monday, 1952. Left to right, the drivers are Alan Brown, Eric Brandon, Juan-Manuel Fangio (in John Cooper's prototype car) and Mike Hawthorn. Immediately behind Fangio, wearing white overalls, is Cooper Senior. To Charlie's right is Jimmy Richmond, patron of Brown and Brandon, and to Jimmy's right is Charlie's twin sister, Judy. John Cooper sits on the tail of Hawthorn's car, to John's left is Mike's mechanic and to the mechanic's left is Elsie Cooper, Charlie's wife and John's mum.

reasons not unconnected with market value. The works also built a prototype Cooper-Bristol sports car with a body resembling the one Vignale built for the Ferrari 212, and at least one customer bought the rolling chassis of a Formula Two car with the intention, from the start, of building it into a sports car. The converted Formula Two cars ran mainly in Britain and the best were very good indeed by the lights of British 2-litre racing, which was a closely contested category with the likes of Frazer Nash, Lister, Tojeiro, Lotus (from 1954) and even the odd Maserati.

Alan Brown was the first to convert a Formula Two car – in fact it was the ex-Hawthorn car. Alan was entered by Hawthorn's old patron, Bob Chase, and, among many successes, he won the 1954 British Empire Trophy and, in the same year, the 2-litre race at the (sports car) Dutch Grand Prix meeting. His car is one of the few to survive as a two-seater.

In 1955 Cooper built a Mk I Formula Two chassis to form the basis of a sports car for private entrant, Sid Greene, which used the 2-litre engine from his A6GCS sports car, but the 'Cooperati' was not a great success. The Italians were fond of quoting wonderful horsepower figures, but when those horses crossed the English Channel, and were tested on a dynamometer, they all seemed to turn into ponies.

Cooper's excursion into Formula Two had begun on a high note with Hawthorn at Goodwood, but there was no development in either the car or the engine, and Cooper stood still while everyone else made advances. Cooper still had ambitions, however, and planned to enter the new 2½-litre Formula One.

CHAPTER THREE

SPORTS CAR CLIMAX

Cooper's never-to-be Formula One car would have used a Coventry Climax V8 engine in what was basically a Cooper-Bristol chassis, in other words, a front-engined design – there was no thought then of breaking the mould. The main business of Coventry Climax was fork-lift trucks, industrial engines, and fire pump engines but, in the early 1950s, its chief engineer was Wally Hassan who had a long and distinguished association with motor sport, and he had recruited Harry Munday from BRM.

A government contract for a light and powerful fire pump engine designated 'FW' (feather weight) had helped Climax become fairly prosperous and, when the 2½-litre Formula One was announced, the head of the company, Leonard Lee, was able to listen sympathetically as Connaught, Cooper, HWM and Kieft approached him with a joint plea to supply them with an engine with which to go Formula One racing. Since he did not have the full backing of his board, Lee insisted that it should be a semi-secret project and so the designation FPE (fire-pump engine) was chosen as an in-house joke, but it has usually been known as the 'Godiva'. Hassan and Munday decided on a dohc short-stroke V8 of 2477cc. It was a compact, light (340lb) engine and, by 1953, was producing over 250bhp with exceptional torque and a wide power band.

Alas, Coventry is a long way from anywhere and although Climax had a potential world-beater on its hands it believed the exaggerated power claims of Italian makers and thought it would be shown up. Thus the best engine of its day – it was superior even to Mercedes-Benz – was never released. But, before the end of 1954, an adaptation of the FW fire pump engine would appear in racing – at Le Mans in a Kieft – and Cooper would build a car to accept it.

While most of the company's output continued to be Formula Three cars, 1954 saw the first Cooper-Jaguar (T33) which was the result of a commission from Peter Whitehead, a gentleman amateur driver of uncommon skill and experience. He was one of Enzo Ferrari's first customers, had driven in Grands Prix and, in 1951, shared the winning Jaguar C-type at Le Mans. Whitehead's idea was to make better use of the Jaguar engine's power with a chassis that would be lighter and would handle better than the C-type. Suspension followed traditional Cooper practice with transverse leaf springs and telescopic dampers, but it had double wishbones front and rear. Disc brakes, then still something of a novelty, were fitted all round and the finished car had similar dimensions and weight to the Jaguar D-type, which was then nearing completion in Coventry.

At the time a number of designers were experimenting with weight distribution, inspired by Piero Taruffi's twin-boom 'Tarf' record car. Nardi and Pegaso both built cars with the driver in one pod and the engine in the other. While the Cooper-Jaguar was not as outlandish as that, the driver sat far to the right, outside the main chassis

Cooper, Kieft and Arnott all went after 500cc international records. Cooper's streamlined record cars were also raced and George Wicken ran this car at Silverstone in 1954. The body of the streamliner became the basis for the T39 Manx Tail Cooper-Climax sports racers.

tubes (it was a multi-tubular frame with a tubular backbone centre section), while the nominal passenger seat was equally far to the left.

Even in Whitehead's hands the car had a fairly lacklustre career: a win in the Wakefield Trophy in Ireland against thin opposition and an undistinguished third in the Oporto Grand Prix, two laps down from a pair of works Lancias, were the highlights of the year. Other cars were sold to a couple of British drivers and one of them, Cyril Wick, was reasonably successful at club level.

1955 saw a revised Mk II version (T38), with more conventional bodywork and seating – achieved by narrowing the central backbone section. It also had a 250bhp dry-sumped version of the engine and, undeterred by his experiences with the Mk I, Whitehead bought one. The highlight of its career came when he ran it at Le Mans with his half-brother, Graham, but it retired after three hours when running fourteenth.

Peter Whitehead returned to Oporto that year and motored steadily to finish fourth in a thin field – and, in the equally low-key Lisbon Grand Prix, the Cooper ran in third place before retiring with transmission trouble. It next appeared in the Tourist Trophy, but retired after forty-four laps with a broken chassis – a very rare occurrence for a Cooper. Whitehead took it to New Zealand that winter and after he raced without particular distinction in the 'International' races, he sold it to Stan Jones (father of 1981 World Champion, Alan Jones) who had better fortune in Australian events. Tommy Sopwith also bought a Mk II and initially planned to fit a Blackburn-Turboméca gas turbine engine. When he got impatient of waiting for the engine to be delivered he settled for a Jaguar unit, but he raced it only occasionally

Leading Trials driver and constructor, Mike Cannon, converted a 1949 Mk III 500cc chassis into this pretty MG-powered GT with an aluminium body by Williams & Pritchard. It is pictured at Brands Hatch in 1954, and is believed to survive in substantially original condition.

TPD 1 was a Mk I Cooper-Bristol converted to a sports car by Tony Crook who ran it with great success. By 1955 it had passed to A.P. 'Bert' Rodgers who re-bodied it and gave it the nickname 'Mucky Pup'. Rodgers is seen here at Goodwood in 1955. Sadly, this very popular driver was to lose his life at the circuit early the following year when he crashed his new Tojeiro-Bristol.

Alan Brown had this one-off Maserati-engined Cooper for the 1955 British GP at Aintree. Nicknamed the 'Cooperati' it was built for Syd Greene's Gilby Engineering and was also raced by Roy Salvadori. It has to be regarded as a failure, however, largely because the engine did not deliver its claimed horsepower.

Jack Brabham ran a T39 fitted with a Bristol engine in the 1955 British GP at Aintree. The car was finished on the morning of the race and Jack ran without a clutch. He had been lapped several times before the engine dropped a valve on lap 31. The car ran well subsequently and was one of many Coopers that Jack took Down Under on his annual visit home.

before changing his racing policy. A third car went to Michael Head (father of Williams designer, Patrick Head), who used it on the road and in British club racing.

The Cooper-Jaguar was not a success. John Cooper and Owen Maddock were out of their depth: they were competing against the likes of Ferrari, Maserati, Jaguar and Aston Martin. Charlie Cooper suspected as much all along, and did not give the project his wholehearted blessing.

In Formula Three, Cooper was still the dominant force even though the class existed only in pockets round the world. America was just waking up to it, and it was strong in Australia and New Zealand. A number of outfits had attempted to market rival cars, but they enjoyed only spasmodic success. At the end of 1954, Cyril Kieft sold his company and returned to the steel industry. Don Parker became a Cooper driver.

THE 'MANX TAIL'

If the Jaguar-powered cars had been flops, Cooper's next sports car redressed the balance. The Coopers had been quick to see the potential of the Coventry Climax FWA engine and they decided to build a Climax-powered sports car for 1955. The performance of the Costin-bodied Lotus Mk VIII had convinced them of the desirability of an aerodynamic shape and they had already produced a 500cc record-breaking car fitted with a streamlined body designed by Owen Maddock.

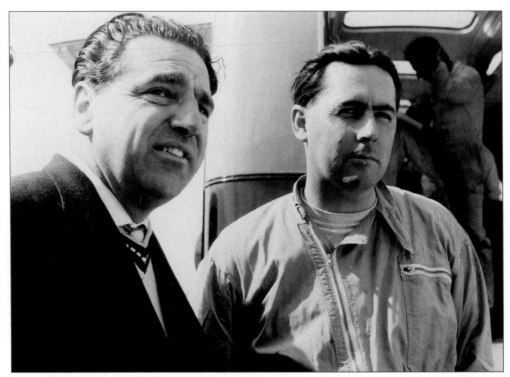

One of the greatest partnerships in motor racing history: John Cooper and Jack Brabham. Jack was more than just a driver, he made an incalculable contribution to the design and development of the cars and John was wise enough to listen.

Coopers rarely ran in World Sports Car Championship events, but the private T39 Manx Tail of Edgar Wadsworth and John Brown ran at Le Mans in 1955 and finished third in the 1100cc class.

John Cooper knew an aerodynamacist at Hawker Aircraft who took a drawing of the record car to his boss for comment. His boss suggested that the overall shape would be suitable for a racing car, while cutting off the tail behind the back wheels and making the rear panel slightly concave would give an aerodynamic advantage and make the car more practical – for one thing it required less room in a transporter.

Having arrived at the shape, John Cooper and Owen Maddock made a simple multiple-tube frame with curved tubes to go beneath it. Because the 500cc record car was mid-engined, this sports car would be mid-engined. Because the driver of the record car sat in the middle, the sports car would have a central driving seat with a passenger seat, fit for an undernourished midget, to the driver's left. This solution also aided the rigidity of the chassis – which is undermined by an open cockpit area. As with most previous Coopers, suspension was independent all round by transverse springs and lower wishbones but there were new cast magnesium alloy wheels which were soon nicknamed the 'bunch of bananas'.

The gearbox, in unit with the final drive, was the French ERSA four-speed conversion of the three-speed Citroën gearbox used in the Traction Avant. There was no other suitable gearbox for a mid-engined car, which is one reason why mid-engined cars were slow in catching on. The gearbox was obtained on a trip to Paris by a new arrival at Cooper Cars: John Arthur 'Jack' Brabham.

Back home in Australia Jack had raced the 'Redex Special' which was a Cooper-Bristol. As well as being a driver, Jack had run his own small engineering business so he fitted the ethos at Cooper since he was prepared to roll up his sleeves and get stuck in. Nicknamed 'Black Jack' – it rhymed and he always had a five o'clock shadow on his chin – Brabham was a taciturn man but, as he proved later when he

The first of three T33 Cooper-Jaguars was commissioned by Peter Whitehead, but it was outclassed at international level. Like some other makers in the early 1950s, Cooper experimented with weight distribution and the driver was so far to the right that he was almost out of the car. Whitehead sold UBH 292 to Cyril Wick (pictured at Ibsley in 1955) who enjoyed success in club racing.

ran his own team, he was a very shrewd operator, none sharper. Unlike Moss who laid back in the cockpit, a position he had originally adopted because it looked elegant, Jack crouched over the wheel and liked to twitch out his car's tail. He gave the impression of driving at the edge of disaster. It was a residue from his days as an Australian dirt track champion and some people slightingly called it 'the village blacksmith school of driving'. That never bothered Jack. Only once in his Formula One career did he sustain an injury that kept him out of the next race – and that was through an accident caused by a tyre failure during a test session. He would take three World Championships, twenty-seven Formula Two races (only Jochen Rindt, on thirty-one, won more), and be the only driver to win the World Championship and the European Formula Two Championship in the same year. He must have been doing something right.

It was a tiny car, with an overall length of 10 feet 10 inches, a wheelbase of 7 feet 5 inches, and a dry weight of just under 900lb. When asked to explain the sawn-off tail, John Cooper described the theory and said he called it a 'Camm tail', for it had been done at the suggestion of Hawker's great designer, Sir Sydney Camm. By an extraordinary coincidence, it fitted the aerodynamic theories of the German scientist Dr Wunibald Kamm, so in print it has generally been called a 'Kamm tail', which is also correct. Its official designation was 'T39', but nobody ever referred to Coopers by their type numbers and in Britain it was usually known as the 'Manx

Peter Whitehead also took delivery of the first (of three) T38 Mk II Cooper-Jaguars. He ran it at Le Mans in 1955, sharing the driving with his half-brother, Graham. After three hours the car was black-flagged for spewing oil. It was later sold to Stan Jones (father of World Champion, Alan) who won many races in Australia with it.

Tail', after the Manx cat which has no tail. Only in recent years has the American nickname, 'Bobtail', become used on both sides of the Atlantic.

When the car was announced, drawings of it appeared in *The Autocar*. Jack ripped one out of the magazine sketched on it in ink and sent it to a friend in Australia. When he next returned home he called by and picked up the drawings and a step gear cluster – this enabled the engine to be mounted 3 inches lower in the frame. Jack's friend was Ron Tauranac, who himself would arrive in England in 1960 to set up Motor Racing Developments with Brabham, and Ron would design the cars which, more than any other make, would force Cooper out of the production racing car business.

For 1955, works Cooper-Climaxes were run for Ivor Bueb and Jim Russell, both graduates from Formula Three, and the first customer car went to Tommy Sopwith who fitted a 1500cc Connaught engine. Since the car cost just £1,350, other customers soon arrived at Surbiton.

It was impossible to know in 1955 that the 1100cc sports car class in Britain was witnessing a significant battle as the Cooper took on the Lotus Mk IX. It was the first time that the two makes had met head on. Lotus's Colin Chapman tended to be dismissive of the Cooper's pragmatic approach and he muttered words like 'bloody blacksmiths'. On the other hand when Owen Maddock once suggested building a stressed and triangulated spaceframe in the Lotus manner, John Cooper had retorted,

YPK 400 pictured at Castle Combe in 1967. The third of the three cars went to Colonel Michael Head, father of Williams design chief, Patrick, who used it for Continental touring as well as racing. Cooper-Jaguars were fine for club events, but out of their depth in even national events. Charlie Cooper was sceptical of the project all along, and he was proved right.

'And be up all night welding it back together again like Chapman has to do?'

There was an element of truth in each man's view of the other – Cooper built for strength, Lotus built for lightness – but, on balance, 1955 was Cooper's year with a large number of wins and places. Most of these were in British club events, but they included class wins in the Goodwood Nine Hours (Ivor Bueb/Jim Russell), the International Trophy at Oulton Park (Russell) and the Tourist Trophy (Bueb/Mike MacDowell), while the privateers, Wadsworth and Brown, finished third in class at Le Mans.

The Coventry Climax engine was light, powerful, reliable and readily available. In a very short time the 1100cc sports car class became the class for the aspiring driver and, equally as quickly, Formula Three declined in importance. Moreover, the 1100cc category gave firms like Cooper and Lotus a firm footing in the USA as they demolished imports from Italy with their crude chassis and Fiat-based engines. Eric Brandon decided that the class was more suited to him than Grands Prix had been and he had his mechanic design a car for him. The mechanic was 'Ginger' Devlin. The car itself, called the Halseylec, was not a great success and the project faded when Eric became more interested in hydroplanes. Ginger returned to Cooper.

A Bristol-powered Manx Tail was entered as a Formula One car for Jack Brabham in the British GP, when it was said to have a 2.2-litre engine. This was not strictly true: it had a standard 1971cc engine, but the RAC turned a blind eye to the fiction to allow the car an entry. There have been times when French and Italian organisers have been said to have turned a blind eye to oversized engines used by favoured teams, but to turn a blind eye to an *undersized* engine must be uniquely British. In the Grand Prix, it was comprehensively outclassed, but it had a couple of decent runs in minor events later that year before going to Australia. A similar car was sold to Bob Chase, but his driver, Mike Keen, crashed it at Goodwood and died.

In 1956, an 1100cc Manx Tail won its class at Sebring and another came eighth overall and second in class at Le Mans. Overall, however, the cars were no match for the new Lotus Eleven – partly because the Eleven was a superb car, partly because Cooper did not have the same aggressive programme as Lotus. Chapman plucked the best young talent for his cars, offered them packages that were hard to refuse and his accountant, Fred Bushell, had to make economic sense of the deals. The Coopers, by contrast, kept a close watch on the balance sheet.

In private hands, Cooper Manx Tails still managed a fair number of wins in British and American club racing in 1956. That same year, however, when fitted with Coventry Climax's 'stop-gap' 1460cc sohc FWB engine, and driven by top-class drivers,

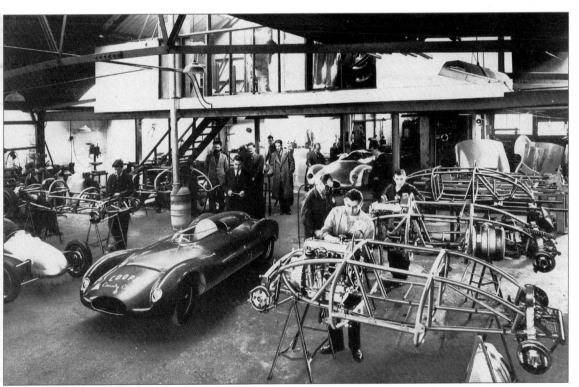

The Hollyfield Road works, 1955, with production of the Cooper T39 Manx Tail in full swing. John Cooper stands behind a car used both for racing and display, hence the helpful sign-writing on the bonnet. Though primitive by modern standards, the Cooper works made hundreds of cars and all to a very high standard. It changed the face of motor racing and played a major part in making Britain the dominant force in the sport.

The start of the Madgwick cup for Formula Two cars at Goodwood on 26 September 1953. On the far side is Roy Salvadori (Connaught A-type), Stirling Moss (no. 7) is in a Mk II Cooper-Alta entered by the works and he has the drop on Tony Rolt (Connaught) and Bob Gerard (Cooper-Bristol). The

head of Les Leston, driving an 1100cc Cooper-JAP, can just be seen to Rolt's right and, behind Leston, is Ken Wharton (Cooper-Bristol). The race was won by Salvadori from Moss, Rolt, Gerard, Wharton and Leston. In Formula Two, Cooper stood still in 1953 while everyone else made advances.

More conventional than the Mk I Cooper-Jaguar, this T38 was first delivered to Tommy Sopwith, son of the great aviation pioneer, who intended to fit a Blackburn-Turbomeca gas turbine engine. That was slow in coming so Sopwith settled for a Jaguar XK unit. All Cooper-Jaguars were fitted with Dunlop disc brakes and Dunlop's alloy wheels with knock-off hubs.

Manx Tails were quite successful in sports car races. Roy Salvadori took two outright wins at the 1956 Easter Monday Goodwood meeting, a win at the International Trophy Meeting at Silverstone, and the City Cup in Oporto, Portugal. Salvadori was third in a race at the Nürburgring, Jack Brabham finished second in the Imola sports car Grand Prix, and Stirling Moss won the British Empire Trophy at Oulton Park.

A new Formula Two, for 1½-litre cars, was scheduled for 1957 and the Coopers set to work to make a car for it. Basically all they did was to take the Manx Tail and narrow it. The chassis was still not a properly triangulated spaceframe but, rather, the curve of the tubes followed the lines of the body.

Although Formula Two would not officially come into being until 1957, an F2 race was included in the British Grand Prix meeting in 1956. Virtually every entry was a sports car, but Roy Salvadori arrived in his Cooper T41, a pukka single-seater. 'Salvo' had little difficulty in winning from Colin Chapman driving a Lotus Eleven, with Ivor Bueb hard on Chapman's heels in a 1½-litre Manx Tail. Salvadori followed that with wins at Brands Hatch, Goodwood and Oulton Park, where five new Coopers were entered. Cooper was about to enter its period of greatest success.

Keith Greene, briefly a Formula One driver, later a leading team manager, enters Woodcote Corner in the 1500cc sports car race at the 1957 Easter Monday Goodwood meeting. Keith finished twelfth and the race was won by Colin Chapman's Lotus Eleven. Note that what was later the 'Super Shell' building then bore the name of National Benzol.

By 1957 production of the Manx Tails had reduced to a trickle. One reason was some of the new rules for international events conspired against the centre-seat concept; another was that as customers turned to Lotus for their sports racers so Cooper turned to the new Formula Two. Though the Manx Tail's successful period covered just two seasons, it was the direct forebear of the car with which Jack Brabham won the 1959 World Championship and led the mid-engined revolution in single-seater racing.

Cooper Cars opened a racing drivers' school in 1957 and made two Manx Tails with conventional seating and an open cockpit. It was not the first racing school by any means, but it was the first with a famous signature. It did not last very long and it did not fulfil its promise to find and groom future champions, but one of the instructors was Jim Russell and he went on to found a school that did find and groom champions. But Cooper had already done that in a different way. Formula One drivers like Stirling Moss, Cliff Allison, Peter Collins, and Stuart Lewis-Evans had cut their teeth in a Cooper Formula Three car – as did Graham Hill. Le Mans winners Ivor Bueb and Ninian Sanderson had done the same. Bernie Ecclestone won races in an F3 Cooper – the long-term influence of the little cars cannot be underestimated.

CHAPTER FOUR

REAR-ENGINE REVOLUTION

Cooper had stolen a march when Formula Two officially started in 1957 simply by getting its car in production before anyone else. That's how it had tackled Formula Three as well – Cooper always had a quick response time. Cooper's career in the four-year span of the 1½-litre Formula Two paralleled the Formula Three experience: it dominated by weight of numbers, won most races, was challenged by others who, for a time, appeared to have the upper hand, but met the challenge and came out on top.

The great thing about Cooper was that it got things done. It was eccentric, but effective. Tony Marsh, six times an RAC Hill Climb Champion and a privateer in Formulae One and Two, recalls, 'My family business was pork products and Charlie simply loved York ham. I'd arrive at the works, produce the biggest York ham you've ever seen, and waft it under Charlie's nose. I'd then tell him that I was going to camp in my transporter and live off the ham. Any that was left when my car was

Jack Brabham swings through the Goodwood chicane – officially Paddock Bend, but nobody ever called it that. Jack brought his T43 home fourth behind two Connaughts and a BRM in the 1957 Glover Trophy. The rear-engine revolution had yet to start.

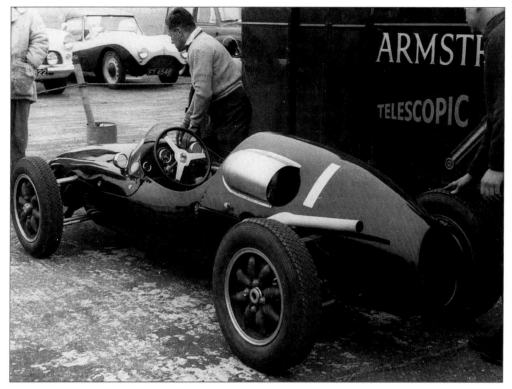

The very first rear-engined Formula Two Cooper was entered for Roy Salvadori in a 'Formula Two' race supporting the 1956 British Grand Prix. Since the new formula would not come into operation until 1957, the rest of the field was sports cars and Roy took an easy win.

finished would be his. You'd be surprised how quickly my car was finished.' Other drivers who enquired where their new car was were sometimes pointed to the tube racks. It sounds amateurish, but cars were usually delivered on time. Charlie ruled the factory with an iron rod, always conscious of cost and profit. He was right; if a racing car maker is not making money, pretty soon it is not making racing cars.

The first official Formula Two race was the Lavant Cup at Goodwood. Cooper had refined the T41 and entered T43s for its works drivers, Roy Salvadori and Jack Brabham. What exactly the differences were between a T41 and a T43 is hard to say – but the bodywork on the T43 was more rounded, particularly the nose cone. Cooper gave very slight variants new type numbers whereas other makers would have added a 'B' to the number or ignored it altogether.

As in the 1956 races, a fair number of sports cars appeared on the grid for the Lavant Cup, but it included two new Lotus 12 single-seaters. For years some of the volunteers who helped Colin Chapman, and who contributed greatly to Lotus's success, had urged that he should built a mid-engined single-seater, and a monocoque at that, but Chapman stubbornly refused in case he appeared to be copying Cooper. So the Lotus 12 was front-engined with all the attendant problems of fitting the driver and the prop shaft in some sort of harmony. If a designer put the driver over the prop shaft there was a penalty in drag. If the prop shaft was routed along the driver by transfer gears, there was a penalty in friction.

Jack Brabham working hard in the 1957 International Trophy. He finished second in his heat, but retired in the final.

Maurice Trintignant was not only a double Grand Prix winner, and a winner at Le Mans, he was also Mayor of Versage, the source of Perrier water. 'Trint' won the 1958 Monaco GP in one of Rob Walker's Coopers and was Stirling Moss's team-mate in the Walker team for 1959.

Roy Salvadori's Cooper expired on the line near the end of the 1957 British Grand Prix at Aintree. While John Cooper, in his trademark hat, investigates, Roy takes light refreshment. Shortly afterwards Stirling Moss went by in the Vanwall to score Britain's first World Championship win while Roy pushed his car across the line to be classified fifth.

Many of the cars had the new twin cam Coventry Climax FPF engine, a unit which was to transform the face of motor racing. It was virtually, and ironically, one block of the aborted 'Godiva' V8, and delivered 141bhp with excellent reliability and torque.

The Lavant Cup itself was won by Tony Brooks in a Cooper entered by Rob Walker, with Brabham's works car second and Ron Flockhart in a 1500cc Lotus Eleven sports car third. Brabham also ran his car in the Formula One Glover Trophy and finished fourth.

Cooper then entered cars for Brabham and Les Leston in the Monaco Grand Prix. Leston's was in Formula Two spec and he failed to qualify, but Jack had a 1960cc FPF, developing 176bhp – the official figure for the Lancia V8 used by Ferrari was 285bhp. Despite this vast difference, the Cooper proved reasonably competitive, being nimble around the tight street circuit. Still, having Formula Two fuel tanks meant that Jack had to stop for fuel but, in a race with many retirements, the little car was lying an amazing third behind Fangio (Maserati) and Brooks (Vanwall) until, on the very last lap, a fuel pump attachment failed. Jack pushed his car to the line to be classified sixth – but sixth place still did not win a Championship point.

After that, Cooper would enter one or two cars in every Grand Prix, and some non-Championship events. The only point it scored was for Salvadori's fifth place in the British Grand Prix at Aintree, which saw Moss and Brooks share a Vanwall to take the first all-British World Championship win. The Coopers had a massive power deficit over the opposition and the whole team was on a steep learning curve.

Start of Heat Two of the 1957 International Trophy with Harry Schell's BRM (no. 7) on pole. Also in the picture are Henry Taylor (Lotus no. 32), Jack Fairman (Cooper no. 26) and Keith Hall (Lotus no. 50). Schell had an easy win, but then most of the opposition was running 1500cc engines.

John Cooper managed the team, but it was his first year in Formula One and everything was new, from booking the hotels to learning the circuits. Formula Two, however, became Formula Cooper and Coopers won every F2 race save two. One was at Reims where Ferrari entered a front-engined car for Maurice Trintignant and he lapped the entire field. Reims, however, was an ultra-fast circuit, more or less three long straights and three corners, and the Ferrari's power was overwhelming. The other Cooper defeat was in the German Grand Prix at the Nürburgring where the organisers included a consecutive Formula Two class. At the 'Ring, the Cooper team's inexperience soon became evident – they had never raced on a circuit with so many swoops and bumps, and both Brabham and Salvadori retired with broken wishbones.

Following the invasion of Egypt by Britain, France and Israel the previous November, and the blocking of the Suez Canal, petrol rationing had been restored for much of 1957, which caused the cancellation of several races. The International Trophy was therefore run in September rather than on its traditional date in May. The only works Formula One team to arrive was BRM with cars for Jean Behra, Ron Flockhart and Harry Schell, but Tony Brooks in Rob Walker's 2-litre Cooper put the cat among the pigeons when, during practice, he lapped a full second ahead of the field. His crown wheel and pinion broke on the starting line, and BRM scored an easy 1–2–3, but Brooks had issued a warning.

For 1958, Cooper adopted a new front suspension by coils springs, double wishbones, and an anti-roll bar so that the car could be more precisely set up for individual circuits. At the time very few drivers possessed the sensitivity to set up a car with precision, but Jack had that ability as did Bruce McLaren who would later join the Cooper works team. To see if the spring rates were right, mechanics would often push down the car at the back and count the number of bounces. Jack, however, had his eye on the ball and knew that Cooper was in danger of losing the initiative. Cooper's advantage was its layout, but the engineering was crude. If someone like Chapman designed a mid-engined car, it could be a serious threat.

John Cooper and Jack had become very close friends and, to a certain extent, co-conspirators. The problem was Charlie who was resistant to any change. Yet the experience of undertaking World Championship races had taught John and Jack that change was necessary.

Production Formula Two cars had disc brakes as standard whereas, previously, they had often had drums. This may seem to be an example of arch-conservatism, but many drivers preferred drum brakes because they were more progressive and predictable than early disc brake systems. Porsche, indeed, did not use discs until mid-1961.

ON THE F1 WORLD STAGE

The Argentine Grand Prix, which opened the 1958 World Championship season, was too far away for Cooper to enter (or Lotus, BRM or Vanwall, come to that), but Rob Walker sent his 2-litre Cooper for Stirling Moss. New fuel regulations specified petrol of up to 130 octane – Av-gas aviation fuel. Ferrari and Maserati had previously used alcohol-based fuel and were having problems in adapting, but the Coventry Climax FPF had been designed from the start to run on petrol.

A straw in the wind. For the International Trophy, Tony Brooks was in Rob Walker's T43 fitted with a 2-litre Coventry Climax engine. Tony put the car on pole 1.6 seconds ahead of eventual winner, Jean Behra in a BRM – and Behra was 1.4 seconds ahead of his fastest team-mate. In heat one, Brooks's final drive failed on the line but, a few months later, Stirling Moss used the same Cooper to win the Argentine GP.

Maurice Trintignant won just two World Championship events and both were at Monaco – in 1955 and 1958. On each occasion, Maurice won because he brought his car home intact while the front-runners fell by the wayside. Here, in

1958, he delivers Cooper's second World Championship win in a Rob Walker Cooper. It was in recognition of this triumph that Cooper named its new sports car the 'Monaco'.

The 1957 German GP at the Nürburgring had a Formula Two class. In qualifying Jack Brabham (pictured) was second fastest to Edgar Barth's stripped-down Porsche RSK sports racer. Barth went on to win the class while Brabham retired.

The circuit in Argentina was abrasive and it was clear that Moss would have to have a tyre change and, with bolt-on wheels, this would cost him considerable time. Moss qualified only seventh on the ten-car grid, but the heat in which the race was run affected the cars recently converted from running on alcohol. Moss plugged away and, on lap thirty-five of eighty, he took the lead. The Ferraris, who by then were the main opposition, were content to let him go, knowing that he had to change wheels – and his mechanics made a great show of getting fresh wheels ready.

Too late Ferrari realised that Moss was not going to stop. He began to drive on the oiliest part of the track to preserve his tyres. Luigi Musso's Ferrari made a late charge but, at the flag, Moss was 2.7 seconds ahead, with the canvas showing on both rear tyres. It was the first World Championship win for Cooper, the first for Dunlop tyres, the first for a mid-engined car, and the first for Coventry Climax. It was also one of the greatest drives in history, combining as it did sheer cunning and Moss's sublime skill.

Ferrari sent a car for Hawthorn to drive in the Glover Trophy at Goodwood and Mike obliged with a win, but Brabham and Salvadori were second and third. Moss, in Rob Walker's Cooper, set joint fastest lap with Hawthorn before a con-rod let go in the engine. Then Moss won the BARC 200 at Aintree with Brabham second and Brooks third, and winner of the Formula Two section. Coopers dominated the entry list and Jean Behra's BRM would run no higher than second to Moss before retiring with brake trouble. The three Maserati 250Fs and the three Lotus 12s struggled.

Tony Brooks, one of the greatest talents in motor racing history, drove Rob Walker's T41 to victory in the 1957 Lavant Cup at the Easter Goodwood meeting. It was the first official Formula Two race to be held to the 1½-litre formula and a Cooper win set the pattern for the four years that the formula ran.

BRM and Ferrari both sent cars for the 1958 International Trophy at Silverstone, which had a very rich entry. Peter Collins won for Ferrari, but Salvadori brought his Cooper home second, ahead of Masten Gregory's Maserati and Behra's BRM. Cooper was making people sit up and take notice though Cliff Allison won the Formula Two section for Lotus, one of the few successes the front-engined cars would achieve.

For Cooper's second visit to Monaco, four cars were entered. Brooks took pole in his Vanwall from Behra's BRM, but next up were the works Coopers of Brabham and Salvadori, and Trintignant in Rob Walker's car. They qualified ahead of all the Ferraris, and all but one Vanwall and one BRM. Only two of the seven Maseratis qualified – yet only the previous year Fangio had won Monaco and taken the World Championship in a Maserati. It was a race with many retirements, first Behra led, but retired. Moss and Hawthorn then swapped the lead, but both retired, and the surprise winner was Maurice Trintignant in Rob Walker's Cooper. Cooper had therefore won the first two World Championship races of the year and 1958 was the first year of the Constructors' Cup, so Cooper was leading that, too.

Brabham had a 2.2-litre engine for Monaco, but the Coopers would only become fully competitive when they received not just enlarged 1½-litre Climax FPF engines, but the bespoke 2½-litre Mk II unit which was then close to readiness. Coventry Climax had stretched the original unit to its absolute limit, 2207cc, partly by putting a spacer between the top of the block and the cylinder head. They made just four of these 194bhp units for the sole use of the Cooper and Lotus works teams. Normally

Alf Francis, Rob Walker's chief mechanic, tends Maurice Trintignant's Cooper T51 prior to the 1959 Monaco GP. Trintignant's car was fitted with Borrani knock-off wire wheels for the race in case a stop for tyres was necessary.

one car in each team would have a 2.2-litre unit, while the other engine was rebuilt back in Coventry, and drivers would take it in turns to use the bigger engine.

The rest of the Formula One season did not live up to the promise of the opening races. Still, it became usual to see at least one Cooper in the front half of the grid, with Cliff Allison's Lotus 16 'Mini-Vanwall' not far behind. The Lotuses, though, were very fragile. Once, after practice at Monza, one needed more than forty individual welds to restore the cracked chassis frame.

Moss won the non-Championship Caen Grand Prix in Rob Walker's Cooper, but the next significant race was the German Grand Prix. Both Cooper and Vanwall had had an unhappy time on their first visit to the 'Ring in 1957, but they returned with modified suspension. On the twists and turns of the 14.7 mile circuit, Coopers were expected to do well. Aided by the fact that Moss and Hawthorn retired after each had been in the lead, and that Peter Collins crashed (fatally, alas) when lying second, Roy Salvadori and Maurice Trintignant brought their Coopers in second and third behind Tony Brooks' Ferrari and ahead of the Ferrari of Wolfgang von Trips.

Moreover, in the concurrent Formula Two section, a teenager fresh from New Zealand, Bruce McLaren, defeated entries from Lotus, Porsche and Ferrari and also finished fifth overall. McLaren would soon find a permanent place at Cooper and he fitted the bill perfectly, being both a fine driver and gifted natural engineer. Together with Jack, he would help Cooper to its period of greatest success. Looking back, John Cooper says, 'I've often been asked if I wouldn't have preferred to have Moss driving for me, but Stirling never won the World Championship and Jack won it twice with us. It's obvious I made the right decision.'

No further successes came Cooper's way in Formula One in 1958. Hawthorn won the drivers' title by a single point from Moss, in the final round at Casablanca, and then promptly retired, devastated by the death at the Nürburgring of his close friend, Peter Collins. The following January he lost control of his Jaguar saloon on the Guildford bypass and was killed.

Vanwall (51 points) won the inaugural Constructor's Cup from Ferrari (45) with Cooper third on 32 points well clear of BRM (18), Maserati (7) and Lotus (5). It had been an astonishing performance by the little team, but Cooper still had not definitely proved the case for a mid-engined layout. It had, however, done enough to get people thinking.

Vanwall withdrew, having won its Championship, and Moss was a free agent again. He elected to drive for two teams. Rob Walker would provide him with a Cooper, but the British Racing Partnership, founded by Stirling's father, Alfred, and manager, Ken Gregory, would prepare a BRM. Stirling therefore could choose between having his engine in front or behind him.

Jack Fairman adjusts the mirrors on his Cooper before the start of his heat in the 1957 International Trophy.

Cooper came close to a clean sheet in Formula Two in 1958. Cliff Allison won for Lotus at Silverstone and Jean Behra's Porsche took wins at Reims and the Avus track in Berlin, both ultra-fast circuits. Winners for Cooper were Maurice Trintignant (Pau and Charade), Stirling Moss (Goodwood), Tony Brooks (Aintree), Bruce McLaren (Silverstone, Brands Hatch and the Nürburgring), Ian Burgess (Crystal Palace and Snetterton), Stuart Lewis-Evans (Brands Hatch), Henry Taylor (Monthléry), Syd Jensen (Crystal Palace), Tim Parnell (Silverstone) and Jack Brabham (Brands Hatch and Casablanca).

Several points can be teased from that list. One is just how many British drivers are on it, a thing almost unimaginable when Cooper first entered Formula Two with the Bristol-engined car only six years previously. Another is that Cooper, as in Formula Three, was capable of providing a car many drivers could win in. The third is how many Formula Two races took place in Britain – Silverstone alone staged three – and how many circuits there now were in the UK. Ten years previously, the only permanent circuit in Britain had been Goodwood, now they were spread throughout the country and those listed were supplemented by lesser venues and temporary airfield circuits. Jim Clark made his début in England at Full Sutton airfield near York. It was used on just four occasions, all in 1958, and is now a maximum security prison, but it played its part.

By now Cooper had virtually stopped making Formula Three cars. The category had died on the Continent after 1953 and, as the 1100cc sports car class became important in 1955, Formula Three went into rapid decline in Britain. Coopers still dominated but Formula Three races featured at major meetings less and less.

The Manx Tail was also now obsolete but, just as the original T41 Formula Two car had been essentially a narrow Manx Tail with open-wheel bodywork, so the next sports car would be essentially an F1/2 car widened with a full-width cockpit. The Monaco which would go through a number of versions, would also be Cooper's last sports car. In style it closely resembled the Cooper Racing Drivers' School Manx Tails and although it was designed to take Coventry Climax FPF engines from 1½-litres to 2½-litres, it was hardly bigger than the Manx Tail (at 7 feet 7 inches, the wheelbase was just two inches longer). It was first shown in late 1958 and it was called the Monaco (T49) in honour of Trintignant's win in the 1958 Monaco GP. Stirling Moss had opened the score in Argentina, but 'Buenos Aires Autodrome' does not roll easily off the tongue.

Cooper built the Monaco solely as a customer car and eight were delivered in 1959. Most stayed in Britain where they were very successful – they clearly had the edge over the front-engined Lotus 15, but then Monacos were driven by the likes of Moss, McLaren, Salvadori, Russell and Brabham and the Lotus 15 did not attract an array of talent like that. Most cars had the 2-litre FPF engine (the 2½-litre version was in short supply and earmarked first for Formula One) but two cars had Maserati engines: the John Coombs car, which was usually driven by Salvadori, and the Monaco owned by the Italian team Scuderia Centro-Sud. They were rarely competitive with the Climax-powered cars, which not only saw off opposition from Lotus, but which would consign all front-engined sports racers, regardless of engine size, to the history books.

CHAPTER FIVE

WORLD CHAMPIONS

The biggest change to the Cooper works team in 1959 was that Roy Salvadori decamped to Aston Martin. Roy was already a works Aston Martin sports car driver, but the company was planning to enter Formula One and the terms it offered beat Cooper's modest retainer. In the event, the Aston Martin DBR4 was an unmitigated disaster, obsolete before it ever raced. It was a bulky front-engined car that showed only one glimmer of promise, when Roy brought one home second in the International Trophy at Silverstone – a race won by Jack Brabham's Cooper.

Joining Jack in the Cooper team was Bruce McLaren, just turned twenty-one, and the American, Masten Gregory, a. driver capable of producing stunning drives, but not consistently. The works Coopers in 1959 had rear upper wishbones to provide better location to the transverse leaf spring and Jack had one of the new 2495cc Coventry Climax FPF Mk II engines. Designed by Wally Hassan and Peter Windsor-Smith, it gave 240bhp, which was nearly 20 per cent more than the interim 2.2-litre FPF. The Climax engine was remarkable. It was strong, reliable and had excellent torque. It may not have been as powerful as those from Ferrari and BRM, but somehow the performance of those cars never convinced one that they really did have 20 per cent more power than a Cooper-Climax.

Jack Brabham sits on the grid at Aintree for the 1959 British Grand Prix. Jack set pole and led the entire race. Wins do not come better than that.

Jack Brabham's Lowline Cooper T53 leads Innes Ireland's Lotus 18 in the 1960 Belgium GP. Jack went on to score the second of five successive World Championship wins. The race was marked by tragedy – Mike Taylor and Stirling Moss had huge accidents in qualifying when parts on their Lotus 18s broke; Chris Bristow and Alan Stacey both died in the race itself.

Roy Salvadori and Bruce Halford were entered in Coopers by Tommy Atkins's High Efficiency Motors for the 1960 Monaco GP. With the field restricted to sixteen starters, Halford missed the cut while Roy's race came to an end just before one-third distance when his car retired with an overheated engine.

In 1959, the German Borgward company released some of its 1½-litre sports car engines for use by Rob Walker and the British Racing Partnership. The four-cylinder Borgward unit was fuel injected and was the first postwar engine to have four valves per cylinder. Pictured is Ivor Bueb's BRP car at the Easter Monday Goodwood meeting. BRP's cars were really successful only when Chris Bristow drove.

It won on its début, when Moss led home Brabham in the Glover Trophy at Goodwood. Tony Brooks and Jean Behra then took a Ferrari 1–2 in the BARC 200 at Aintree, but only after the Coopers of Gregory and Moss had both taken turns at leading. Moss's car was fitted with a four-cylinder BRM engine, mated to a new gearbox made by Valerio Colotti in Italy. It was typical of Moss that he would be looking for an advantage and the Cooper-BRM was not merely one engine taken out and the other put in. The chassis and suspension had to be modified considerably and the result was unstable so it raced just the once.

The mid-engined Coopers would be fitted with all manner of engines – Alfa Romeo, Alta, Aston Martin, Bristol, BRM, Connaught, Ferrari, Ford, Maserati, OSCA, and the 'Arden' (a Butterworth AJB bottom end fitted with Norton barrels and heads). None of them was successful; Cooper and Climax seemed to go together like eggs with bacon.

Having 240bhp from the new FPF engine was welcome, but it made the Ersa transmission marginal – it was after all, derived from a Citroën road car unit. In fact, by 1959, it had evolved into a Cooper-Knight gearbox. Cooper (i.e. Jack Brabham) had been developing it in conjunction with Jack Knight – today the world's major supplier of steering racks.

Moss's only flaw as a driver was that he was prone make unnecessary changes and the Colotti gearbox was one. Moss had met Colotti when he had driven for Maserati and Colotti had been the company's transmission specialist. He had left Maserati when they withdrew from racing at the end of 1957 and had established his own design studio, Tec-Mec. Colotti's gearbox was a sound design – Colotti 'boxes would later be used by Cooper – the problems started when it came to put it into production. Around Cooper and Lotus there had started to spring subcontractors who would form the backbone of the British motor racing industry. Neither Cooper nor Lotus made their own engines or transmissions, and both bought in many other components. Italian companies like Ferrari and Maserati tended to make everything in-house, so there was no network of subcontractors. Colotti had to farm out the components for his transmission and they came back ineptly made. Moss retired from the race at Aintree with a broken gearbox and this was to be the first of several failures. The Colotti transmission probably cost Stirling the World Championship; it certainly led to an unjustified reputation as a car breaker. Those more kindly disposed to him referred to a 'Jinx' and this was taken up with gusto by sections of the popular press. You do not, however, win more than 220 races by being a 'car breaker'.

For the World Championship opener at Monaco, Moss took pole in his Cooper, Jack Brabham was third, and sandwiched between them was Jean Behra's Ferrari. Behra led until lap 21 when his engine went sick. Moss and Brabham were by in a trice and led easily until, after eighty-one laps, Stirling's gearbox gave up. So Jack went on to a win the first World Championship victory for himself, the works Cooper team and the new Coventry Climax engine,

Jo Bonnier gave BRM its first Championship victory in the Dutch Grand Prix. The Swede had been on the pace throughout the meeting, but Moss was actually ahead when his gearbox gave up. Jack came home a strong second to consolidate both his and Cooper's positions at the top of their respective Championship tables. In third place was Masten Gregory in another works Cooper – he took points for himself, but only the top finisher of a make scored for the Constructors' Cup. Ferrari bounced back at Reims with Tony Brooks leading home Phil Hill for an emphatic 1–2, with Jack in third place. Stirling had elected to drive the British Racing Partnership's BRM while his mechanic, Alf Francis, tried to sort out the problems with the Colotti gearbox. The race was run in torrid heat. Stirling lost the car as the track began to melt and he couldn't get it started again.

With Ferrari and BRM both winning races, the case was still not proven for a mid-engined layout. True, Ferrari had won at Reims, where sheer power was at a premium, but Behra's Ferrari had led at Monaco where a Cooper was expected to have the edge. When asked about mid-engined cars, Enzo Ferrari had loftily said, 'From time immemorial the horse has pulled the cart, not pushed it.' It was one of those daft sayings the man was prone to – from the mid-1950s, mid-engined Porsches with half the engine capacity of a Ferrari had managed to win endurance sports car races outright. Perhaps the case hadn't been quite proven, but Ferrari quietly bought a pair of Coopers during 1959 to evaluate. They were fitted with Ferrari four-cylinder engines, tested and then appeared in a couple of minor races under the name of a wholly fictitious team called Scuderia Eugenio Castellotti, in honour of Italy's last driver of potential greatness.

Industrial disputes in Italy meant that Ferrari missed the British Grand Prix at Aintree, where the team had scored a decisive 1–2 earlier in the year. Moss's gearbox still had not been sorted so, once more, he was in the BRM. Jack led the race from flag to flag, with Stirling second and McLaren third – the only cars to complete the full distance. Harry Schell in a works BRM was fourth, but Coopers were fifth and sixth – four cars in the top six. McLaren had sensibly been playing himself in during the season as he came to terms with learning the craft of a Grand Prix driver, but by mid-season he had reached the stage where he could offer full support to his team-leader.

For some reason it was decided to run the 1959 German Grand Prix at Avus – a banked track in Berlin where, in 1937, streamlined Mercedes-Benz and Auto Union Grand Prix cars had lapped at over 170 mph. The race would be a high-speed thrash and was the only World Championship race ever to be run in heats. There were two, with the winner decided on aggregate times. It promised to be a Ferrari walkover, and so it proved with Brooks winning from his team-mates Dan Gurney and Phil Hill. Everyone else struggled and the best of the rest was Maurice Trintignant in a Rob Walker Cooper in fourth place and lapped. The retirement rate was high. None of the three works Coopers finished, while Moss went out after two laps with a broken gearbox – again.

Missing from the Ferrari team was Jean Behra who had had a king-sized row with the Ferrari management over their refusal to nominate him as team leader. The

In 1960 the private Yeoman Credit/British Racing Partnership team ran Cooper T51s with distinctive bodywork. The three cars entered for the Portuguese GP line up in the paddock awaiting their drivers – Tony Brooks, Olivier Gendebien and Henry Taylor. The cars effectively went backwards throughout the season and, at Oporto, even the great Tony Brooks could finish only fifth, six laps down.

Tony Brooks at Monaco in one of the Cooper T51s run by the British Racing Partnership in 1960. He had just left Ferrari since he wanted to live in England and wind down his racing activities. Tony qualified third behind Moss and Brabham and eventually brought his car home fourth.

brave, if mercurial, Frenchmen was snatched by BRM, but they didn't have a car ready for the German GP. If they had had one, Behra wouldn't have accepted an offer to drive a Porsche in a sports car race at Avus the day before the Grand Prix. The race took place in heavy rain, Behra crashed at high speed and was killed.

As the Grand Prix circus went to Portugal, the World Championship appeared to be a two-horse race with Brabham on 27 points and Brooks on 23. At the time Moss was on 8½ points – there was a point for fastest lap and he'd shared that at Aintree. Stirling was not about to give up, however, and during practice he demonstrated why he stood head and shoulders above his rivals.

He reckoned that the best times would be set towards the end of the practice period when the air and road began to cool. The big drawback was that the sun would be low and there would be sections of the track where it shone directly into his eyes. The solution was simple, he drove those sections one-handed with the other hand shading his eyes. Incredible though it may seem, Moss set pole position more than 2 seconds ahead of Brabham. Third on the grid was Masten Gregory – the first all-Cooper front row in a Championship race. Moss sailed into the lead and lapped the entire field – the only time it has been done in a World Championship race in the dry. Second was Masten Gregory, which was to be his highest ever Championship finish. Jack crashed (something most unusual for him), after tangling with a backmarker he was lapping. The car was wrecked, but Jack was back in action for the Italian Grand Prix three weeks later.

The Italian race took place at Monza and incorporated the high-speed bankings that had been rebuilt in 1955. This was a ploy obviously designed to favour Ferrari, who

Bruce McLaren, the youngest driver ever to win a World Championship Formula One race, was an enormous asset to Cooper both as a driver and as an engineer. He was also one of the best-liked men in motor racing.

were confidently expected to repeat their dominance. One problem with using the bankings was the high tyre wear rate they generated, and Ferrari knew that it would have to make a pit stop. Coopers still had bolt-on wheels so a change of tyres would put them out of the running. When the cars arrived at the circuit Moss's Cooper was fitted with wire wheels at the rear – a clear indication that he knew he would have to stop.

Stirling set pole from Brooks and Brabham and was content to run second to Phil Hill's Ferrari. When the Ferraris were called in to change tyres, Stirling was firmly in the lead, and in the lead he stayed. He had been able to obtain a set of tyres – made by Dunlop for road use – which had a deeper tread than usual. The wire wheels had been a bluff, and Stirling ran to the finish without stopping and secured the Constructors' Cup for Cooper. Phil Hill finished second with Jack third.

With one round of the Championship remaining the position was Brabham 31 points, Moss 25½ and Brooks 23 – but only the five best scores counted so if Jack finished second in the United States Grand Prix at Sebring, he would score 6 points, but would have to discard 4 points for one of his two third places so would have a nett gain of two. Brooks did not have to shed any while Moss had a couple of points for fastest laps to drop. Any of the three could take the title.

In the event, Brooks was rammed from behind on the first lap and he called to have his car checked. That delayed him, but he would fight his way back to third,

Bruce McLaren (Cooper T53 Lowline) on his way to second place in the 1960 Monaco GP. The T53 was an outstanding design which rarely gets the credit it deserves.

Roy Salvadori's name was synonymous with Cooper from 1956 and he eventually became the team manager. Roy was an immensely glamorous figure and one of the great stars of British motor racing in the 1950s and early 1960s.

Stirling, who had led from pole, retired after five laps with another broken gearbox. Jack then led but, a lap from the end, his car ran out of fuel. Not for the first time he pushed it home, arriving absolutely exhausted in fourth place. The irony is that the fourth place had to be deducted from his final score, and as a result his efforts were in vain so far as his tally was concerned. He was World Champion without the effort. As Jack slowed, Bruce McLaren shot into the lead to come the youngest winner of a Formula One World Championship race in the history of the sport, aged 22 and 104 days. And Cooper won the Constructors' Cup from Ferrari, BRM and Lotus. The 'blacksmiths' from Surbiton had taken on the world's best and beaten them.

Had Brooks not stopped to have his car inspected, he would probably taken the title. In fact, Tony had been unlucky on two counts. The first was that the Belgian Grand Prix was cancelled, and Tony was the supreme master of the demanding Spa circuit which was ideally suited to his Ferrari. Then Ferrari missed the British Grand Prix – and Ferrari had scored a 1–2 at Aintree earlier in the year. As for Moss, he would say after he retired that he was much better known for being the greatest driver not to win the Championship than he would have been had he only won it once or twice.

FORMULA TWO DOMINATION

Formula Two continued to be a Cooper benefit with races falling to Jack Brabham (Goodwood and Brands Hatch), Jim Russell (Oulton Park and Silverstone), Mike Taylor (Aintree), Stirling Moss (Syracuse, Reims, Rouen and Clermont Ferrand), Jack Lewis (Monthléry), Tim Parnell (Silverstone and Mallory Park – twice), Maurice Trintignant (Pau), Roy Salvadori (Crystal Palace), Stan Hart (Edzell), Ron Carter (Silverstone), Chris Bristow (Aintree, Brands Hatch and Snetterton), Henry Taylor (Whitchurch), Tony Marsh (Zeltweg), Trevor Taylor (Rufforth) and Harry Schell (Monthléry).

In fact, every single Formula Two race held in 1959 fell to Cooper. As in 1958, there was wide spread of winners. To be sure some of the races were little more than club events, but others were packed with Grand Prix stars. The wins taken by Chris Bristow and Stirling Moss are interesting since both used four-cylinder Borgwards engines. This German company held a similar position to Audi today, but went into liquidation in 1961. The engine Moss and Bristow used, apart from being fuel-injected, was the first postwar design to feature four valves per cylinder. It was used in Formula Two only during 1959, but the two men won seven races between them.

The Cooper Monaco kept Cooper's name alive in sports car racing. McLaren and Jim Russell drove the latter's car at Le Mans and it was in ninth place, with a chance of winning the 2-litre class, when Russell was involved in a huge accident not of his making and the car was destroyed. Jim had had a long relationship with Cooper and had taken a hat-trick of Formula Three Championships, 1955–7. He had begun 1959 in fine style at Oulton Park winning the British Empire Trophy in his Formula Two Cooper and the Unlimited Sports Car Race in his Monaco – and every British driver except Moss was there. The crash at Le Mans ended Russell's career, just as he was preparing to take a serious stab at Formula One.

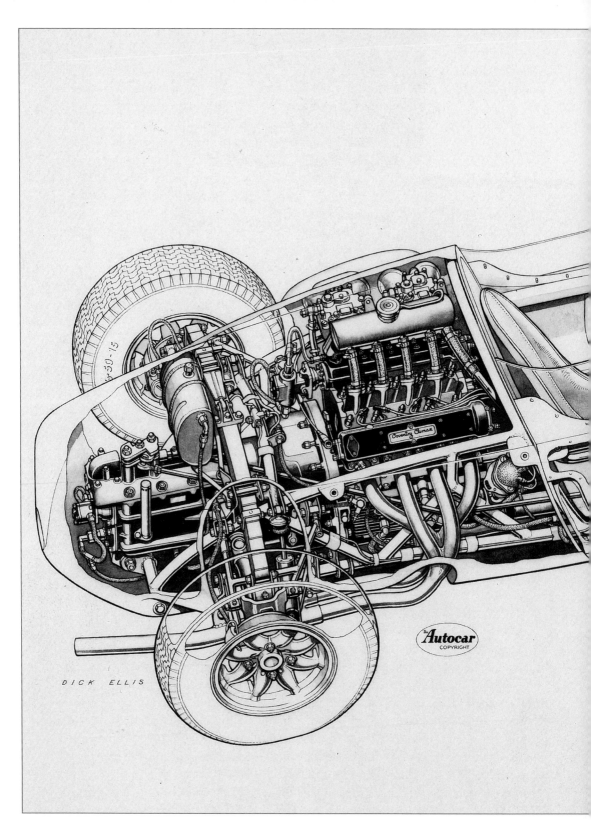

DICK ELLIS

A Cooper T51 exposed. The T51 was used by the works in 1959, and offered as a customer car in 1960. The chassis frame still has curved tubes, so is not a properly triangulated spaceframe. On the other hand, the gauge of

the tubing and the hefty brackets meant that breakages were almost unknown and the old adage has it, 'to finish first, you've first to finish'. Though the T51 was tightly packaged, its successor, the T53 Lowline, was even smaller.

There were two other significant developments during 1959 which would impact on Cooper. In 1959, Formula Junior, which had been an Italian national category, became an international class and replaced the old 500cc Formula Three as the bottom rung on the single-seater ladder. That wiped out Cooper's Formula Three market and production dropped from twenty-five cars in 1958 to four in 1959.

At Monaco, a Formula Junior race supported the Grand Prix. John Cooper and Jack Brabham looked at the cars, which were mainly front-engined and looked like Maseratis in miniature, and decided to build a Cooper for the new class. Formula Junior used production car components. John Cooper had become friends with BMC's chief designer, Alec Issigonis, when they competed in hill climbs just after the war – John in his 500cc Cooper, Alec with his Austin 7-engined Lightweight Special (a monocoque design which used rubber as its springing medium). They admired each other's approach to design and met frequently. John Cooper recalls:

We had to use a production engine, I knew Issigonis, but didn't know anyone at Ford, so it was natural we should go to BMC. Issigonis introduced us to Eddie

When not driving for Aston Martin in Formula One in 1959, Roy Salvadori was entered by Tommy Atkins in a Cooper-Maserati. This photograph, taken at Reims where Roy retired with a broken piston, shows the installation. The Maserati engine, a four-cylinder unit derived from the 250S sports car, was never on the pace with the Coventry Climax FPF.

Maurice Trintignant's own Cooper T45 Formula Two car at the 1960 Syracuse Grand Prix. Trintignant's great gift was bringing his car to the finish and, while faster runners fell out. At Syracuse, 'Trint' was a strong second to the Ferrari of Wolfgang von Trips.

Maher, who ran Morris Engines at Coventry, and who was a motor racing enthusiast. We reached an agreement whereby BMC would supply us with Series-A engines, bored out to 994cc. There was work done on the cylinder head, with bigger valves and stronger springs, a nitrided crankshaft and a twin-choke Weber 45 DCO E carburettor.

During my visits to the works, I saw the Mini prototypes and, a few days after it was launched, Issigonis lent us one of the pre-production cars to use as a team tender at the Italian Grand Prix.

John had to transport a Formula One car to the race (towed behind his Ford Zephyr) so Roy Salvadori was delegated to drive the Mini to Monza. To say that Roy was impressed by the car is an understatement. He covered the distance to Monza quicker than Reg Parnell – and Parnell was driving an Aston Martin DB4GT, then one of the world's fastest cars. The Mini was out of breath at 70 mph, but its road holding was outstanding.

Since the Mini was new, it attracted considerable attention. Aurelio Lampredi, formerly Ferrari's chief designer, but then a senior engineer with Fiat, asked if he could drive it. John Cooper recalled, 'He was gone for hours and we were convinced he'd had a major accident – we'd have some explaining to do and it wouldn't be good for the Mini's image. Eventually he came back, grinning from ear to ear. He

The Tyrrell transporter says everything there is to say about this shot except that Surtees raced in Formula Junior only once. After that and a couple of Formula Two races (second at Oulton Park, fourth at Aintree)

John was in Formula One.

Keith Ballisat in a Team Tyrrell Cooper leads Brian Hart's Terrier in the Formula Junior race at the 1960 British GP meeting. Ballisat was not to progress much higher, but Hart went on to become a leading driver in Formula Two and a notable builder of engines.

Hill climb expert, Ray Fielding, used to travel from Forres in the north of Scotland for his few seconds up venues like Prescott where he is shown here on his way to winning the RAC Sports Car Hill Climb Championship in 1960. Since his Monaco is road-registered, and has head rests for both driver and passenger, it seems likely that it was in active use on the roads of Morayshire.

Mike Spence on his way to victory in his FJ Cooper Mk I at Silverstone in 1960. Mike would go on to drive in Formula One for both BRM and Lotus and Colin Chapman considered him to be one of the outstanding drivers of the 1960s. He was killed in a Lotus while practising for the 1968 Indianapolis 500.

said, "This is the car of the future. If it wasn't so ugly, I'd shoot myself!"' Within two years, BMC would launch the Mini Cooper and it would become one of the most desirable cars in the world, driven by rock stars and royalty. And it was raced with great success by the Cooper works under the management of Ginger Devlin.

The Cooper Formula Junior car was a typical Cooper design, more or less a scaled-down version of the 1959 F1/2 car with its curved-tube frame and suspension coils springs at the front and a transverse leaf spring at the rear. The first fully-supported FJ race in Britain occurred at Brands Hatch on Boxing Day 1959 and it seemed that every specialist maker had a new car to show. Elva, the sports car specialist, had a front-engined design with the works cars powered by three-cylinder two-stroke DKW engines from Germany. Lola had a neat front-engined design with Ford power. Jim Clark made his single-seat race début in another front-engined design, made by a new outfit called Gemini. Also making its début was the Lotus 18, Colin Chapman's first mid-engined design. With its boxy body and solid alloy wheels someone described it as a shoe box with four dustbin lids attached. It didn't show too well in the race either: the Ford Anglia engine, which was the first tuning work carried out by the newly formed Cosworth Engineering, developed a fault and a standard cylinder head had to be substituted. Then the suspension settings were wrong and its driver, Alan Stacey, spun twice.

The race was won by an Elva, with another in third place and a Lola was sandwiched between them. Front-engined cars filled the top three places and the new Lotus looked to be no threat. Cooper, however, went away to prepare for 1960 feeling quietly confident. Not long into the season that confidence would be shattered.

CHAPTER SIX

TOP OF THE WORLD

The Cooper factory was buzzing over the winter of 1959/60. Though Formula Two had only one more year to run, it would become Formula One in 1961 so there was no reason not buy a car. Just as Formula Two cars became Formula One cars on 1 January 1961, so Formula Two races became Formula One events, often calling themselves Grands Prix. Orders were also coming in for Formula Junior cars and there was a Mk II edition of the Monaco sports-racer.

Cooper's defence of its World Championship title began in Argentina where Moss set pole in his Rob Walker car, but alongside him was Innes Ireland in a new Lotus 18. Ireland took the lead at the start, spun down to sixth on lap 2 and lay second at half distance. Moss and Brabham had both retired by this time. Ireland led in the closing stages and then fell back with gear linkage problems. The race went to Bruce McLaren, his second Grand Prix in succession, but the performance of the new Lotus shook Cooper and Brabham and they knew that when they returned to England, there was work to be done.

Back at Surbiton they placed a seat on the floor and arranged tubes around it to see how narrow they could make the new car. It was to become the T53 'Lowline' – the first Cooper with a straight-tube frame. Against Charlie Cooper's protests, suspension would be by coil springs and double-wishbones all round.

Jack Brabham had been in touch with Ron Tauranac, who was preparing to join him in England to start a new company. Ron replied by letter laying down the parameters of the suspension geometry to guide Owen Maddock. The Cooper team landed back in England from Argentina on 16 March and the first 'Lowline' was to race on 6 May – a remarkable feat.

By inviting Tauranac to join him in a new venture, Jack had already decided that Cooper had no future. Motor racing was becoming ever more scientific, and science was unknown in Surbiton. The problem was Charlie Cooper, who couldn't see that things were changing. In fact, Jack and Roy Salvadori had once discussed the possibility of buying Cooper out. Their worst fears were confirmed at Goodwood in March when Jim Clark, having his first drive in a Lotus, beat the Cooper of John Surtees who was having his first drive, period. Then at the Easter Monday Goodwood Meeting, Ireland beat Moss twice in an afternoon – Stirling drove a Cooper in the Formula One Glover Trophy and a Porsche in the Formula Two Lavant Cup.

It made headlines in the national press, just as Mike Hawthorn had done at Goodwood eight years earlier. Then Ireland won the International Trophy from Brabham's new Lowline, with Graham Hill third in the new mid-engined BRM. Stirling Moss, never one to ignore an advantage, had a Lotus for the Monaco Grand Prix where he set pole from Brabham and Chris Bristow. Bristow, considered an outstanding prospect, was paired with Tony Brooks in Coopers run by the British

Reg Parnell (Racing)/Yeoman Credit produced this 'streamlined' T53 for Surtees at the 1961 Dutch GP at Zandvoort . . .

. . . in the race he preferred his regular T61, which he brought home seventh.

First lap of the 1960 Monaco GP. Jack Brabham has the nose of his Lowline ahead of Tony Brooks (no. 18) and Tony's team-mate, Chris Bristow (no. 16). Coming up on the inside is Moss in Rob Walker's new Lotus 18. The handful of photographers and officials certainly had a superb view of the race, which has actually enjoyed an

excellent safety record despite the lack of protection in the picture. Moss went on to score the first World Championship win for Lotus from Bruce McLaren (Cooper), Phil Hill (Ferrari) and Brooks.

Bruce McLaren (Cooper-Climax T55) in the Silver City Trophy at Brands Hatch in 1961. The race was one of twenty non-Championship F1 events held that year and it attracted all the top teams and drivers with the exception of Ferrari. Bruce was in fifth place when he crashed after being forced off line by a backmarker he was lapping.

Jack Brabham in the same race had a less happy time than his team-mate. For some reason he was off the pace in qualifying and his race ended at about half distance with a broken cam follower.

Racing Partnership. Surprise, surprise, Ferrari had a new mid-engined car for Richie Ginther, making his début for the team. (After the race it was put away and Ferrari concentrated racing on his front-engined cars, while developing a new mid-engined design.) Bonnier's mid-engined BRM figured strongly early in the Monaco race, but it was Moss at the flag to give Lotus its first World Championship win, with McLaren second in his Lowline and now leading the Championship.

Moss harried Brabham in the Dutch Grand Prix, but one of Jack's rear wheels dislodged a piece of kerbing which smashed one of Stirling's front wheels. It cost Stirling nearly two laps in the pits so while Jack went on to an untroubled win, Stirling had to tiger to finish fourth behind Brabham, Ireland and Graham Hill. The first four cars were all mid-engined, with the highest Ferrari fifth and lapped.

Then came the Belgian Grand Prix. In practice Mike Taylor crashed his Lotus 18 when the steering wheel came adrift – he never raced again and later sued Lotus successfully. Then a rear stub axle broke on Moss's Lotus, which shed the wheel and causing him serious injuries including broken nose, ribs and both legs. During the race itself, Chris Bristow overcooked things, hit a fence and was killed. Shortly afterwards, Alan Stacey, driving a works Lotus was hit in the face by a pheasant and the impact broke his neck. It was an horrendous weekend, but Brabham and McLaren sailed home to take a 1–2 for the Cooper works. Then, in the French Grand Prix at Reims it was Brabham first and McLaren third with the BRP-entered Cooper of the Belgian, Olivier Gendebien, sandwiched between.

With Moss out of action, Lotus was not looking so bright. Colin Chapman was bringing on two newcomers in Jim Clark and John Surtees. Clark was still feeling his way, however, and Surtees was combining cars with winning a couple of World Motorcycle Championships, so was not available for all races.

Leading American Formula Junior driver, Walt Hangsen, in his 1961 Cooper Mk II running in one of the two Formula Junior races organised that year in Cuba. That was before the Bay of Pigs débâcle.

John Cooper models a new hat at the 1961 Dutch GP. Despite the endorsement of the double World Champion constructor, the style failed to take the world by storm.

The BRMs were looking strong and Graham Hill came close to winning the British Grand Prix at Silverstone. Graham had been second on the grid, alongside Jack on pole, but was rammed at the start and stalled. He set off as Jack sailed away into the distance. Hill worked his way up from twenty-first on lap 1 to second on lap 37 and then to first on lap 55. He had been having problems with his brakes, however, and he spun out of the race on lap 71, five laps from the flag. Hill's misfortune gave Brabham his fourth win on the trot, with John Surtees in a most impressive second place in only his third Formula One race.

Jack won the non-Championship Silver City Trophy at Brands Hatch from Hill and McLaren, then he and Bruce took 1–2 in the Portuguese Grand Prix, Jack's fifth Championship win in succession. Jack took the drivers' title, with Bruce runner-up and Cooper had the Constructors' Cup for the second year, even though there were two races left to run.

There *were* two in theory, but the British teams objected to the used of the Monza bankings. They claimed that the bankings were dangerous because they put undue stress on the cars. Further, they'd be handicapped unfairly by having bolt-on wheels since a wheel change would be necessary and there hadn't been routine wheel changing for years. The real reason was that they knew, as the organisers knew, that given the bankings, Ferrari would walk the race. The Brits had been happy to race on the bankings the previous year, but now they were beginning to flex their muscles. They were already unhappy about Formula One being run to 1500cc in

Bruce McLaren's T55 in the paddock at the Aintree 200 in 1961. Bruce was to finish second to Jack Brabham's sister car. This shot shows the installation of the remarkable Coventry Climax FPF engine.

1961 and launched plans for a 3-litre 'Inter-Continental' formula. The boycott of the Italian Grand Prix had more to do with politics than safety. Ferrari turned up, of course, and finished 1–2–3. It was the last World Championship race to be won by a front-engined car: the Cooper revolution was complete.

It was not only the British and Italians who were being political. In 1960 the German Grand Prix was a Formula Two race. The reason? Porsche had a strong Formula Two car and there was no German Formula One car. At the Nürburgring Porsche duly posted a 1–2, but Jack was third.

Moss had returned to the cockpit in Portugal but, for once, had been fairly lacklustre. In fact he spun and was disqualified for driving the wrong way when he restarted. He put his Lotus on pole for the United States Grand Prix at Riverside, however, with Jack alongside. Brabham took an immediate lead when there was an explosion from the back of his car. He pitted to investigate and lost more than a lap – it turned out that fuel overflow pipe was dripping on to the exhaust pipe. Moss went on to a comfortable lead, followed by Ireland and McLaren, but Jack worked his way up from eighteenth to fourth. Though it didn't result in a win, and the three points he scored were surplus to requirements, it was perhaps Jack's best drive of the season. He had been helped to the title by Moss's absence for three races, but he had not put a foot wrong all year. Further, he had made a significant input into the design of the Lowline Cooper.

With the 1½-litre Formula Two due to become Formula One in 1961, both Ferrari and Porsche began to take it very seriously. As well as running a works team,

Jack Brabham was leading the 1960 Monaco GP when he spun and was subsequently disqualified for receiving outside assistance. The race was won by Stirling Moss who thus gave Lotus its first World Championship victory, as he'd also done for Cooper and Vanwall.

This is a picture that almost needs no caption. It's a Lowline in Rob Walker's colours and the number, is seven. It has to be a Moss car in 1961. It's actually in the paddock for the Aintree 200, run to the Inter-Continental formula, where Stirling had so many problems during practice that he started from the ninth row from ten. Spectators who relished the prospect of Moss slicing through the field were disappointed, his engine gave up after the first lap.

Porsche supplied a car to Rob Walker for Moss to drive, while Lotus had a revised version of the 18.

Cooper could not possibly improve over 1959 when it had won every Formula Two race and the fact it had built the Lowline specifically to compete with the Lotus 18 showed how worried the team was. The existing Formula Two cars, with their curved-tube frames Lowline lines, were obsolete by Cooper's own admission. The final score, however, was Cooper 12 wins, Lotus 6, Porsche 5 and Ferrari 3, but there are lies, damned lies and statistics. Of the 26 events, Ferrari entered only 5, yet won 3 of them. Team Lotus, entered 9 and won 6 and Porsche entered 10 and won 5. Furthermore, most of Cooper's wins were achieved when the grids consisted mainly of Coopers with a sprinkling of old Lotuses. A list of race winners disguises the true position. Cooper won the most races, but was the weakest of the four constructors.

Just as Formula Two was going to be the new Formula One, so Formula Junior was set to be the level of single-seater racing immediately below Formula One, but without the Grand Prix stars who had raced so often in Formula Two. Formula Junior gave all the small constructors and special builders throughout the world a chance to compete on a level playing field. An Italian company like Stanguellini had previously met Cooper or Lotus only occasionally, usually at Le Mans or the Reims 12-Hour race, or when private owners competed in America. With easier travel by 1960, and a European Championship to play for, dozens of small outfits now entered the new arena. It was a chance for everyone to put their ideas to the test. There were cars with engines to the fore of the front-axle line, and cars with engines behind the rear-axle line. There were front-engined cars, mid-engined cars and even one with the engine alongside the driver.

At the end of the season British makers, led by Lotus and Cooper, had established dominance. The Lotus 18 with its Cosworth-tuned Ford engines was the most successful, but Cooper-BMCs were close behind. Indeed, Henry Taylor won the most important Formula Three race of the year, at Monaco, in a Team Tyrrell Cooper-BMC.

Coopers were particularly popular and successful in America where drivers were private owners racing a long way from factory support. American drivers liked a lot of oversteer and this the Formula Junior Cooper provided, in contrast to the Lotus, which needed more precision to obtain the best from it.

British constructors had developed their craft on airfield circuits, with their smooth surfaces, whereas so many Continental races took place on street circuits with cobblestones, potholes, manhole covers and all the rest. Their chassis design had centred on strength, not subtlety. Then again, the power output claims made for many foreign engines, notably DKW and Fiat, were shown to be fanciful. At the end of the 1960 season, drivers had either to junk their front-engined cars and buy British, or resign themselves to not winning. The result was to wipe out the majority of small constructors beyond the UK and, with them, any chance that a motor racing industry would develop elsewhere.

More than anything else, the 1960 Formula Junior season ensured that Britain would become the home of single-seater design. The burgeoning motor racing industry and the success of the leading makes would develop a culture where it would seem natural for a bright graduate to become a racing car designer as it once had been for him to seek a job in the aircraft industry. More than thirty years after Cooper left racing, its legacy can still be found in the modern British motor racing industry.

Driving a Team Tyrrell Cooper Mk I, Henry Taylor had a magnificent win in the Formula Junior race which supported the 1960 Monaco GP. Taylor would graduate to Formula One, but never quite became an obvious first choice.

Jack Brabham, crouched and purposeful, on his way to sixth at Zandvoort in 1961.

A shot showing the back end of a Cooper exposed. This time it's the T53 which Roy Salvadori (right) drove to fifth place in the 1961 Syracuse GP.

Ron Tauranac had arrived in England in the April and found a flat close to the Cooper works. His first job was to engineer the installation of a Coventry Climax engine in a Triumph Herald and Jack Brabham sold about 100 of these through his garage business. In addition to this, Ron was engaged on the design and construction of a first Formula Junior car for Motor Racing Developments, the partnership he had founded with Jack

Jack already had his own independent team, the Brabham Racing Organisation. BRO would enter a Cooper for him in races that the works didn't enter. Cooper's total budget in 1960 was £10,000 – that built two cars – everything else came from bonuses, prize money and starting money. Jack had his own trade deals and he was widely used to endorse products in advertisements.

Because Cooper couldn't afford to pay Jack a retainer worthy of a World Champion, he and Bruce were allowed to take their cars back home to Australia over the European winter. As returning heroes they could command great starting money. When it was time to return to Europe, they sold their cars to local drivers, and the money they made was most of their salary from Cooper. Jack was already semi-independent without the contractual restrictions of a driver today. He was however determined to become totally independent. In short, he saw no future for Cooper while Charlie wielded influence.

John Cooper was privy to Jack's plans and knew there was nothing he could do the change his mind. Charlie was furious. He saw only ingratitude and fumed about 'all we've done for him', but Jack had contributed more than anyone to Cooper's World Championships. The Lowline was cooked up almost behind Charlie's back. So, as Cooper reached the pinnacle of its achievement, with back-to-back World Championships, the team was in the process of being dismantled.

CHAPTER SEVEN

COOPER GOES TO INDY

The British had opposed the 1½-litre formula, confident they could get their own way. When it was clear that there would be no reprieve, both Coventry Climax and BRM were behind with the V8 engines they reckoned would be necessary to beat the Ferrari V6 and the flat-eight Porsche, which was known to be under development.

The 3-litre Inter-Continental Formula was proposed as an alternative and five races were run. Stirling Moss, significantly, decided to race a Cooper Lowline in preference to the Lotus 18 he'd raced in 1960. All the top British teams took part; Moss won three of the five races and Brabham the other two. Modern opinion tends to rate the Lotus 18 more highly than the Lowline, but Jack's five successive Grand Prix wins and the clean sweep of the Inter-Continental Formula suggests otherwise.

For 1961, Cooper's customer Formula One car was the T53 Lowline while the works ran a brace of T55s. These were based on the T53, but the engine was positioned slightly lower in the frame, the bodywork was slimmer – there was less fuel to carry – and it had a Cooper-Jack Knight gearbox.

The season started promisingly with John Surtees winning the Lombank Trophy at Snetterton in a T53, entered by Reg Parnell. Then Jack Brabham put his T53 on pole for the Pau Grand Prix, but he retired with fuel pump failure and Jim Clark won for Lotus. Surtees won the Glover Trophy at Goodwood and Brabham led McLaren home in the Brussels Grand Prix. Moss won the Vienna Cup in his Lotus, but Jack and Bruce scored another 1–2 in the BARC 200 at Aintree. After the first six races of the season, Cooper had taken four wins, Lotus two. So far, so good.

Three days after the race at Aintree most of the leading British runners, plus the works Porsches, ran in the Syracuse Grand Prix. Ferrari's works team was absent, but it had loaned the prototype of its new mid-engined car to an organisation which was the rough equivalent of 'Racing for Britain'. A youngster called Giancarlo Baghetti had been selected to drive the car and, in his first Formula One race, he qualified second, just a tenth of a second slower than Dan Gurney's Porsche. Baghetti was slow away and lay seventh on lap 1, but he was in the lead by lap 6 and won from the Porsches of Gurney and Bonnier. The Ferrari 'Sharknose' had arrived – and how. An unknown driver, in his first Formula One race, and driving the works hack car, had beaten the best drivers in the world. There was a sharp intake of breath.

At Monaco, however, Stirling Moss, in his Lotus 18, put in one of the greatest drives in history to beat off three works Ferraris. Fifth-placed Dan Gurney (Porsche) was twice lapped and Bruce McLaren, in sixth, was lapped five times. Ferrari dominated World Championship races save at Monaco and the Nürburgring, where Moss once again demonstrated why so many aficionados regard him as the greatest of all drivers.

Jack on his way to victory in the 1960 Dutch GP, the first win for the Lowline.

L. Jacobs swings his Cooper Mk III FJ car through Bottom Bend at Brands Hatch in 1962. The picture gives a good idea of just how low and sleek the car was. Formula Junior was the first European category to insist on a roll hoop, but one wonders how effective this one would be, especially since the driver is not wearing seat straps.

Jack poses with the Indianapolis car outside the Cooper works in Langley Road, Surbiton. Note the Dunlop alloy knock-off wheels and the rollover bar – two changes made for America which might also have been useful in Formula One.

A GLIMMER OF HOPE

It was at the Nürburgring that British fans saw a glimmer of hope. As reigning World Champion, Jack Brabham was the first driver to get one of the new Coventry Climax V8 engines. Jack put his revised car, the T58, in second place on the grid, but the conditions were wet/dry at the start and the tyre technology of the time did not embrace 'intermediate' compounds and Jack started with dry tyres at the front and wets at the rear. A mile after the start, he hit a large puddle and finished in the scenery. He would race the V8 car only once more, in the United States Grand Prix, a race which Ferrari missed because it had already taken both World titles. At Watkins Glen, NY State, Jack took pole by more than a second, and swapped the lead with Moss for the first half of the race. Then both retired for different mechanical reasons.

Jack's last race for Cooper produced pole position and saw him lead until forced out by overheating. It was a good way, if not a perfect way, in which to finish a partnership of friends. The United States Grand Prix was finally won by Innes Ireland and was the first World Championship win by Team Lotus. Ireland's reward was to be dropped by Colin Chapman. According to Lotus insiders this was because Innes was more than usually fond of a liquid made in his native Scotland. That was never denied; racing drivers then did not have personal trainers. The trouble was that Chapman was not straightforward with Innes and did not give him the time to find a decent berth. It wouldn't have happened at Cooper.

Stirling's wins and the one by Innes Ireland in America, which Ferrari missed, gave Lotus runner-up position in the Constructors' Cup. Porsche was third and Cooper was fourth. Ferrari had won five World Championship races, and two non-Championship events, while Moss had done the opposite: two Championship wins and five non-Championship victories. Cooper – no fewer than forty-nine Coopers ran in Formula One in 1961 – managed a total of five wins, all in non-Championship races. After back-to-back World Championships, Cooper's best result in the World Championship was Bruce McLaren's third place in the Italian Grand Prix. Jack managed sixth place in the Dutch Grand Prix, and third in the British race, but he retired with car trouble in every other event.

After the bright promise of the early-season races from the end of April on, the best Jack could achieve was a couple of second places in non-Championship races. People began to mutter that Jack had lucked-in to his titles by being at Cooper when it had chanced upon the mid-engined layout. Jack, however, was still winning Grands Prix nine years later; it was Cooper that was in trouble.

Jack was moving away and would not be available to help plan a new car for 1962. The first product of his partnership with Ron Tauranac, the MRD-1 Formula Junior car, made its début in mid-season in the hands of an Australian amateur called Gavin Youl and, from the start, it was clear that it was a superior car. Cars made by Motor Racing Developments would be sold as Brabhams after it was pointed out that MRD is pronounced *merde* in French and what French driver would want to race a car called 'shit'?

This rear view of Jack's 1961 Indycar clearly shows the offset suspension, biased because all corners at Indianapolis are left-handers. Note, too, the 'nerf' bar which was standard fitting at the Speedway.

Jack's Cooper is dwarfed by both the size of the Indianapolis International Speedway and by rival cars.

BREAKING WITH TRADITION

There was a certain amount of turmoil in Surbiton as Jack prepared to leave. But the background was hidden by two major developments for Cooper: Indianapolis and the Mini Cooper. One of the entrants for the 1959 United States Grand Prix had been Roger Ward, winner of both the 1959 Indianapolis 500 and the American Championship. Ward had been persuaded that his Kurtis-Offenhauser quarter-mile midget racer (which complied with Formula One rules) would see off those foreign guys. He was put right during practice when his best lap was 43.8 seconds off the pace and, since Moss's pole time was three minutes dead, practice indicated that Ward could be lapped nine or ten times during the race. He lasted just twenty laps before his humiliation ended with a broken clutch.

Far from being embittered by the experience, Ward took it on the chin and began to work on John Cooper. He persuaded John that he should take a serious look at Indianapolis. Before the 1960 United States Grand Prix at Riverside, Jack drove his Formula One car at the Indianapolis Speedway and the exercise was promising.

Jack set a time which would have seen him ninth on the grid at the 1960 Indianapolis 500, less than 3 mph slower than the man on pole. And Jack was driving a 2.5-litre car while the Indycar formula then allowed cars which were 2.8 litres supercharged, 4.2 litres unsupercharged. Cooper's 'toe in the water' exercise caused quite a stir among the Indianapolis brigade. As word got around, leading

Jack Brabham's Cooper leads Paul Goldsmith in a traditional Indianapolis roadster at the Brickyard in 1961. Despite giving away 1500cc, the speed of the Cooper in the turns tolled the death knell for the front-engined roadster.

drivers and engineers headed for the Speedway to watch the funny little car go faster in the turns than any car had gone before.

Jim Kimberly, racing enthusiast and boss of Kleenex, put up the money (sponsorship was years away in Europe) for Cooper to build a car for the 1961 Indianapolis 500. Cooper adapted a T53 Lowline with a 2.7-litre Coventry Climax FPF engine, specially created for the occasion and tuned to run on a 50/50 mix of petrol and methanol. It drove through a two-speed gearbox, which was usual at Indianapolis. Dunlop knock-off alloy wheels were fitted, the fuel tanks were repositioned because the Speedway has only left-hand turns and, following usual Indy practice, the suspension was off-set (the distance between the wheel and the centre line on the nearside was less than that on the offside). Dunlop supplied tyres with an asymmetrical tread.

It broke with Indianapolis tradition in two respects. First it was called the Kimberly-Cooper whereas most Indycars ignored the constructor and concentrated on the sponsor. You'd have the *Sugaripe Prune Special* and the *Dean Van Lines Special*, yet both could be Kurtis-Offenhausers. The other innovation was that the car was painted traditional Cooper green with two white stripes. There had never been a green car at Indianapolis before and the superstitious were appalled. In one sense they were right to be appalled, because their cosy little world was about to be pulled apart.

Jack was giving away 1500cc, but the Cooper, dwarfed by traditional front-engined Indy roadsters, was two-thirds their weight and considerably faster through the turns. It ran like a train, held fourth position at one point and finally finished ninth. He and John had agreed before hand that a top ten finish would be very acceptable. Jack might have been seventh or, even, sixth, had he and his pit crew been more experienced in the arcane ways of Indianapolis. Formula One had forgotten about routine pit stops and knew nothing about running under a yellow flag.

Even ninth place showered money on Cooper and Brabham, more than they'd ever known from any Formula One race. John Cooper recalls, 'There were all sorts of currency regulations at the time and after a race in Europe we'd be paid in the local currency. Every Monday morning you'd see Jack, Bruce and me doing the rounds of the banks in the Surbiton area changing marks, francs and lire into sterling, £300 at a time.'

Cooper never did return to Indianapolis though the car, which was sold after the 1961 race, did so without success. Jim Clark and Lotus came within a questionable decision by the stewards of winning the race in 1963, but they would win in 1965 when thirty-two of the thirty-three cars on the grid were mid-engined. The one front-engined roadster on the grid in 1965 qualified bog last and retired after one lap.

The Indianapolis adventure was typical Cooper: it broke the mould, set the pace but didn't follow through. Jack had been working his corner, however, and had been talking to team owners about his plans. In the October 1961 he received a draft contract from Paxton Superchargers, a subsidiary of Studebaker-Packard, offering to buy a prototype Brabham Indycar, plus six customer cars, in return for exclusive rights. Paxton guaranteed to buy ten cars a year from 1963 on. It was a deal that makers of production racing cars dream of, but the contract was not completed. Ron and Jack had made only one Formula Junior car at the time and weren't geared up to handle such an order. The idea behind the Paxton contract, however, indicates Jack's ambitions and was thrashed out as he flew between Europe and America during the Indianapolis 'Month of May' when MRD-1 had yet to turn a wheel. It will be noticed that it was Motor Racing Developments which received the overtures, not Cooper. Jack had become merely a driver for Cooper, he no longer had an input to the cars and, hence to the future of the company.

Just after Cooper redefined Indy racing, as it had Formula One, the British Motor Corporation unveiled the first Mini Cooper. By the time it appeared, the Mini had already established a reputation for its outstanding roadholding. The cars were soon snapped up by motor racing people who, since the top speed of early Minis was not much over 70 mph, bought tuning kits for them. Naturally they had been raced and in 1960 the British Saloon Car Championship had been won by John Whitmore in an 850cc Mini.

John Cooper asked Ginger Devlin to modify a Mini. It was the first step for a car which was to become a legend, but Ginger says, 'I remember very little about it. It was a job I fitted in between looking after Jack's Formula One car. I suppose all I did was to tune the engine using bits from our Formula Junior engines.' John Cooper recalls, 'Lockheed was making disc brakes and was keen to get involved. I knew the boss of Lockheed and they fitted disc brakes on the front wheels for us. We also had a remote gear-change. I can't remember, but I suppose Jack Knight made one for us.'

John modified a Mini, but he also had close ties with BMC and was a double World Champion. Lots of people were tuning Minis, but only John could go straight to the top of BMC, to George Harriman. Harriman was mightily impressed with John's car, and the Cooper sales pitch, which centred on the proposition that, if BMC would make

The fabulously wealthy Lance Reventlow (an heir to the Woolworth fortune) dabbled as a racing driver on both sides of the Atlantic before building his successful Scarab sports racers and the antiquated Scarab F1 cars. Scarab was the last team to enter Formula One with front-engined cars, yet Reventlow owned a Formula Two Cooper.

1,000 cars with 1-litre engines, they could be homologated for international racing and rallying. The larger engine was necessary to take advantage of the 1000cc limit on the smallest class, while the disc brakes would be essential for success.

Harriman doubted that as many as 1,000 cars could be sold, but he gave the green light to the project. Harriman was right to be cautious, no British manufacturer had ever offered a special 'speed' edition of a standard saloon, let alone one which was so clearly linked to motor racing. At Harriman's suggestion, Cooper was paid a royalty of £2 per car.

THE BIRTH OF A LEGEND

The Mini Cooper was launched in July 1961 and, at £680, cost about one third more than the basic Austin Se7en – that's how it was spelt – or Morris Mini-Minor. The first Mini Coopers had a 997cc engine, remote gearchange, disc brakes on the front wheels, two-tone paintwork, a distinctive grille and bumpers, and top-of-range interior trim. BMC had no difficulty in selling them. Indeed, the demand was so great that the problem was making them quickly enough to satisfy demand. In the early years, however, the Mini Cooper was a niche car bought by enthusiasts. It was not until about 1966 that it became the preferred mode of transport of royalty and rock stars, who drove 1275cc 'S' models, usually with special 'wood and leather' interiors

Roy Salvadori in the prototype Monaco Mk III at the 1961 International Trophy Meeting where he finished second to Moss in a Lotus 19 'Monte Carlo'. The car was so new it was unpainted while the non-functional rear fins were added to appeal to American customers.

created by specialist coachbuilders. The Mini Cooper legend reached its peak in 1969 with the movie, *The Italian Job*, and the irony is that when the film came out, Cooper was no longer in motor racing. But for the time being, Cooper added a works Mini Cooper team to its programme. Ginger Devlin became the team manager and former Cooper racer, Ken Tyrrell, was also involved as an overlap of his running the works-assisted Formula Junior team.

Cooper had been drubbed by Lotus in Formula Junior in 1960 and the reason was that it had built a car which was superior to everything, made anywhere, except the Lotus 18. However, the 1961 Cooper Formula Junior car, the T56, was made for the job. Slim and low with 13-inch wheels replacing the original 15-inch ones, it was a Lowline on a smaller scale.

Ken Tyrrell ran a two-car works team for John Love from Rhodesia (now Zimbabwe) and the South African, Tony Maggs. They had a fabulous season except when they met the works Lotus 20 driven by Peter Arundell, but then Arundell had the potential to become one of the great drivers until he was involved in an racing accident not of his making. Coopers did well everywhere in Formula Junior in 1961, but did particularly well in America.

Cooper was successful in sports car racing as well, but at national rather than international level. The Mk II (T57) version of the Monaco, which had been raced in 1960, was virtually identical to the Mk I save for a longer nose. Most of the handful made stayed in Britain where they ruled the roost in sports car events, but sports car racing was declining in popularity as people found Formula Junior and GT racing more appealing.

1961 saw the Monaco Mk III (T61) which was based on the 1960 Lowline Formula 1 car – with straight tubes in the frame and, for the first time on a Cooper production car, coil springs (with double wishbones) at the rear. It also had a revised

Jimmy Blumer was a leading light in north of England club racing but his talent seemed to become muted when he got south of the Humber. In 1961 he had a 2-litre Cooper Monaco, but was out of the running at the International Trophy meeting.

body with pronounced tail fins which, it was hoped, would make it attractive to American buyers. The new Lotus 19 was also really a two-seat Formula one car which was nicknamed the 'Monte Carlo' as a complimentary nod to the Monaco and also to commemorate Lotus's first World Championship win. Given a half-decent driver, the Lotus was able to wipe the floor with the Cooper, but few of them were made and their owners did not enter them in a full programme of races.

Cooper began 1961 as the reigning World Champion constructor and ended the year fourth behind Ferrari, Lotus and Porsche. Only BRM fared worse, but then BRM was running tired Coventry Climax engines in cars designed for a 2½-litre engine.

Jack Brabham had steadily distanced himself during the season, which is possibly one reason why Cooper slipped down the order. Charlie Cooper thought him an ingrate for leaving, but had Cooper been more go-ahead Jack might not have left; he was, after all, taking a gamble by bringing Ron Tauranac from Australia. Ron had designed no more than a series of specials called Ralts, named for himself and his brother. Ralt stood for Ron and Austin Tauranac – the 'L' was added so the name wasn't 'Rat'. It was almost as though Michael Schumacher had set up a Formula One team where the chief designer was an old friend who had made some Formula Ford cars. In Bruce McLaren, however, Cooper had an asset both as an engineer and a driver and his influence was to be seen in the T60, the works V8 car for 1962.

There were still plenty of Coopers with four-cylinder engines competing in non-Championship events and occasionally making up the numbers in Grands Prix but, from 1962 on Cooper ceased to be the supplier of Formula One cars to the world. Before it did so, however, in December 1961, it sold a car to the Okura Trading Company in Japan. Okura was a front for Honda, which was planning to enter F1 and wanted to see what made a Cooper tick.

CHAPTER EIGHT

THE CRACKS SHOW

After Jack Brabham left to run his own team, first using a Lotus 24 then a Brabham Formula One car, Bruce McLaren became team leader and Tony Maggs was brought in to support him. Cooper was building new cars to take the Coventry Climax FWMV V8 engines, but progress was slower than usual.

For once, Cooper missed the first two non-Championship events, but Bruce arrived at the 1962 Goodwood Easter Monday meeting with a '61 car. The Lavant Trophy, traditionally for Formula Two cars, was run for Formula One cars with four-cylinder engines and Bruce set pole and won. He ran the same car in the Glover Trophy for all Formula One cars, and finished second to Graham Hill's BRM, which had BRM's

Bruce McLaren and John Cooper at Goodwood in September 1962 with the prototype Monaco-Climax T61M. The car used 1962 Cooper Formula One suspension and the unusual notch front wings were intended to direct air to the engine intakes. Bruce ran it in the lucrative west coast sports car series before selling it to Roger Penske.

Bruce McLaren in the 1962 Dutch GP. He had his T60 up to second place behind Jim Clark's new monocoque Lotus 25 when, at quarter distance, his gearbox failed.

J.D. Palmer's modified Cooper Mk I at Brands Hatch in 1965. Not only has the car been rebodied, but there appears to be an oil cooler under the main air intake and subsidiary coil springs have been fitted at the front.

new V8 engine. It was Graham's first Formula One victory; by the end of the season he would be World Champion.

The Glover Trophy was the race in which Stirling Moss had the near-fatal accident which precipitated his retirement from racing. Still only thirty-two, and younger than Graham Hill, Stirling had played a significant part in Cooper's history. He had won with Cooper in Formula One, Two and Three, and sports cars, and had given Cooper its first World Championship victory. Stirling's contribution to the Cooper story is incalculable. But Stirling languished in a coma while Bruce, still with a '61 car, finished second to Jim Clark's V8 Lotus-Climax 24 in the Aintree 200, narrowly beating the works Ferraris of Phil Hill and Giancarlo Baghetti. Having dominated in 1961, Ferrari was in disarray since most of its senior personnel had left to join the new ATS project. The Scuderia would be a shadow of the force it was in 1961.

In the International Trophy Bruce finished fifth and lapped, but he had the consolation of being the first four-cylinder car home. For the Dutch Grand Prix he had a new Cooper T60 with a V8 engine while Tony Maggs, getting a drive at last, was at the wheel of a '61 car. The T60 was stiffer than before and had higher roll centres (which Bruce preferred). The main chassis tubes doubled as oil and water pipes and, together with Jack Knight Engineering, Cooper came up with a six-speed transaxle – a first for Formula One.

While the new Cooper car was an advance, Colin Chapman suddenly made it, and every other chassis, obsolete at the Dutch GP by unveiling the Lotus 25 with its monocoque construction. The monocoque was not only lighter than the spaceframe it replaced, but was considerably stiffer. The stiffness of the chassis allowed Lotus to run softer suspension settings which were a distinct advantage in slow and medium corners, especially since tyres there were hard. That much would become clear as the car was developed. In Holland it was John Surtees who sprang a surprise by putting his Lola on pole. The arrival of Lola seemed to demote Cooper another place in the standings, but by mid-season Reg Parnell (Racing), which was running Lolas for Surtees and Salvadori, had run out of steam and the cars slipped down the order.

As it was, Clark led the Dutch Grand Prix until he encountered clutch trouble. Graham Hill's BRM won from Trevor Taylor's Lotus 24, Bruce retired with gearbox problems and Tony Maggs came home fifth, two laps down. Since Bruce had been holding second when he retired, the team had cause for optimism. That was rewarded at Monaco, where Bruce won. It is true that both Clark and Graham Hill retired, but McLaren had led the early laps and his speed in the second half of the race had caused Hill to perhaps overstress an engine that was losing oil. It would, however, be the only World Championship victory that Cooper was to enjoy during the five years of the 1500cc Formula One.

The 'World Championship' victory has to be described as the only one in 1962 even though in July, Bruce won the Reims Grand Prix. According to the twisted logic that the World Championship has imposed on motor racing, this win did not count. Reims used to alternate with Rouen for the honour of being nominated as the Grand Prix de l'ACF, or French Grand Prix as it's usually called. Bruce won on a full Grand Prix circuit and over a longer distance than the race at Rouen the following week.

Each year first Jack Brabham, then Bruce McLaren, would return home to Australia during the European winter to take part in the Tasman series. At Goodwood in October 1962 Bruce tested this lightweight T63 fitted with a 2.7-litre Coventry Climax FPF engine prior to shipping it Down Under. At the end of the series it would be sold to a local driver – a way for Cooper to reward its works drivers.

The Tyrrell-run Formula Junior Mk IIIs in the paddock at Snetterton in April 1962. Behind are the works Mini Coopers of John Rhodes (no. 74) and John Whitmore. Cooper had a reasonable year in Formula Junior, but not when Peter Arundell's works Lotus was in the race.

John Taylor put in some fine drives in a Cooper T71/73 fitted with a Cosworth-tuned 1498cc Ford engine entered by Bob Gerard. He even ran the car in some non-Championship F1 races, but is seen here at Mallory Park in a

Formula Libre event. Taylor competed in a handful of World Championship races but, sadly, died of burns after crashing in the 1966 German Grand Prix.

Bruce was on the pace throughout the 1962 Monaco GP. He qualified third, led the opening laps, had tussles with Hill and Clark and finally came through to win. It was the only World Championship victory that Cooper would take during the 1½-litre Formula One, 1961–5.

Not only was every team that ran at Rouen present at Reims, with the exception of Porsche, but there were five additional private entries. The only difference was that one race attracted Championship points that year and the other didn't. But unfortunately, after Reims, it was downhill all the way for Cooper.

Rouen turned out to be a race of attrition and was won by Dan Gurney in a Porsche. (This remains Porsche's only World Championship win.) Maggs, now in a T60, was second, albeit a lap down, and McLaren was fourth, two laps down. Bruce was third in the British Grand Prix with Maggs sixth. They were fifth and ninth at the Nürburgring and a lone entry for McLaren in the Gold Cup at Oulton Park ended when his car caught fire. Like most other works teams, Cooper gave the many non-Championship races a miss because there was a shortage of engines. During the entire 1500cc Formula One, Coventry Climax made only 33 V8 engines, compared to the 75 that Mercedes-Benz built for the 13 races in which it competed in 1954 and 1955.

Bruce ended the season with third places in the Italian and United States Grands Prix, and he and Maggs took second and third in South Africa, the final round of the Championship. It had been a fairly good year. Bruce was third in the Championship behind Graham Hill and Jim Clark and he had actually grossed more points than

Clark, but only the best five results counted. In the Constructors' Cup, Cooper was third behind BRM and Lotus. Had the points been awarded in the way they are in 1999, with both cars eligible for points rather than merely the lead car, Cooper would have been a clear second. As it was, it grossed only one point fewer than Lotus.

Cooper also had a reasonably good year in Formula Junior with a Mk III version fitted with disc brakes and, usually, a 1095cc engine. Formula Junior was run on a capacity/weight basis, but the extra power from the larger engine more than compensated for the 40 kg weight penalty. Ken Tyrrell ran the works team for Tony Maggs (when F1 commitments permitted), John Love and Denny Hulme. They gave a good account of themselves, as did private owners in the USA, but the fly in the ointment continued to be Peter Arundell's works Lotus-Ford. Cosworth was getting up to 10bhp more from the Ford 105E unit than BMC was obtaining from its A-Series engines.

Cooper built twenty-eight FJ cars in 1962 and Tyrrell built his own from Cooper parts, but the customer car side of the operation was in decline. Arundell's success brought custom to Lotus, but a good story was spreading about the new Brabham FJ cars. There were a dozen in the field in 1962 and while they were not clearly

M.F. Budge decides to park his Mk III Formula Junior during a Formula Libre race at Mallory Park in 1963. Like any courteous driver he is anxious to get his car off the racing line.

superior, they won races and customers liked them because they were user-friendly, both on the track and in the paddock when being worked on. Brabham was to wipe Cooper from the customer racing car market.

In Formula One and Formula Junior, then, Cooper had enjoyed a respectable season. Much the same could be said of sports cars. The last car of the Monaco line, the Mk IV (T61M), had a revised frame, the latest F1 suspension, and a more subdued body style. John Cooper was keen to run one for Bruce McLaren in classic long-distance events, but Charlie Cooper was still sore at Jack Brabham's departure and was determined to keep a tight rein on McLaren. One of these cars came fifth at Sebring in 1962, however, and most of the few built went to America where domestic V8 engines were often fitted.

Roger Penske meantime bought one of the 1961 Cooper F1 cars, added the 2.7-litre FPF engine that Cooper used at Indianapolis in 1961, and created a centre-seat sports car, the Zerex Special. By degrees this evolved into an offset sports car

Roger Penske bought one of the 1960 Lowline Formula One Coopers from Briggs Cunningham, fitted the 2.7-litre Climax engine from Jack Brabham's Indianapolis car and created the centre-seat Zerex Duralite Special. It was one of the cars which inspired the growth of 'big banger' sports car racing that led to the Can-Am Championship. This Zerex Special, with Penske driving at Brands Hatch in 1963, was based on the ex-McLaren T61M and had a Chevrolet engine.

Cooper Monacos were fitted with all sorts of engines and Phil Barak's car had a Ferrari unit in 1962. The nose of the Monaco was modified to reflect the twin-nostril (or Sharknose) intake on the contemporary Ferrari Testa Rossa.

Barak's car passed to Chris Summers, a popular figure on the club scene partly due to his gutsy driving, partly due to his penchant for fitting big powerful engines to his cars. At the 1962 Boxing Day Brands Hatch meeting, his Monaco had a Chevrolet V8 engine in the back

with an Oldsmobile V8, which was subsequently owned by Bruce McLaren, and from there it was not too large a step to the McLaren Can-Am cars, the first of which would be designed by Owen Maddock.

1962 saw another string added to Cooper's bow in the form of the Mini Cooper. The works ran a two-car team under the management of Ginger Devlin, while Ken Tyrrell frequently helped out, especially when running abroad. The works drivers were John Love and reigning British Saloon Car Champion, John Whitmore. Daniel Richmond of Downton Engineering was engaged to work on the engines – Richmond was probably the finest tuner of the A-Series engine.

As well as the works cars, there were numerous privateers with cars tuned by the likes of Ralph Broad and Don Moore. With so many strong contenders in the field, it was essential that Whitmore and Love did not take points from each other, so the agreed policy for the works team was that whoever was ahead in the Championship should be backed by the other driver. John Love won the first round so Whitmore was obliged to support him until such time as Love faltered. Love never did falter so Whitmore spent a frustrating season backing his team-mate. At the British Grand Prix meeting, however, Whitmore shot into the lead and pulled away. Late in the race he slowed to allow Love to pass, but he had made his point and felt better for it. He would receive the same consideration from his team-mate the following season. Love took the British Saloon Car Championship for the works team.

Overall, 1962 was a good year for Cooper. There was the third place in both the drivers' and constructors' World Championships, two Formula One wins, successes in Formula Junior and American sports car racing and the British Saloon Car Championship. Furthermore, the road-going Mini Cooper had become something of a cult car in a way which it probably would not have been had it been badged something like 'Mini Sports'. The Cooper name had potency.

However, the decline was about to set in because Charlie still wanted to keep a tight rein on McLaren. It was a short-sighted policy because putting restrictions on Bruce meant that Cooper did not benefit as much as it might have done from Bruce's engineering expertise and it had the effect of hastening the day when he would leave to establish his own team.

CHAPTER NINE

HIGHS AND LOWS

Cooper retained the team of McLaren and Maggs for 1963. Bruce was fourth in the Lombank Trophy at Snetterton and second, with Maggs third, to Ireland's Lotus 24 at Goodwood. Team Lotus was absent from Goodwood, however, and there was only one works Brabham. Had the BRMs of Graham Hill and Richie Ginther remained healthy, they would have cruised to an easy 1–2. A more accurate picture of Cooper's competitiveness was seen at the Aintree 200 where Bruce could qualify no higher than seventh, 2.8 seconds off the pace, and finish a distant fifth. The Cooper was happier at Silverstone where McLaren qualified third and finished second to Clark.

The opening World Championship events were promising. McLaren was third at Monaco (Maggs was fifth, two laps down) and second in the Belgian Grand Prix. It has to be said, however, that the Monaco place was inherited after Clark, Brabham and Brabham's new team-mate, Dan Gurney, all encountered problems and the second place in Belgium was due more to Bruce's talent than to the car. From half distance, the race was run in a thunderstorm and Bruce could really show his skills.

Former World Champion, Phil Hill (Cooper-Climax T73) in the 1964 French GP at Rouen. Phil did not have a happy year with Cooper because, for some reason, the personal chemistry between him and the team was never right. It's one of those inexplicable things, especially since John Cooper and Phil Hill were both men of the utmost integrity.

Jackie Stewart in a Formula Two Team Tyrrell Cooper-BRM T75 leads Graham Hill's (sideways) Brabham in the first heat of the London Trophy at Crystal Palace. Jackie's race ended with a broken con-rod. Graham went on to finish second overall to Jim Clark's Lotus.

George Keylock was another to favour an American V8 engine, this time a 3.5-litre Buick V8 – the unit that would become the Rover V8. Keylock is picture at the Dyrham Park hill climb in May 1963 – individual stub exhaust pipes were popular at the time.

Chris Summers was an immensely popular feature of British racing with his press-on style and his use of American V8 engines. His Cooper-Chevrolet, seen here in a Formula Libre race at Mallory Park in late 1963, was one of the elements that inspired Formula 5000.

McLaren qualified third for the French Grand Prix at Reims, but he retired, while Tony Maggs came through to finish a fine second. The Coopers were sixth and seventh on the grid at Silverstone, but Bruce was an early retiree and Maggs could do no better than ninth, four laps down. Neither driver finished the German GP, though McLaren briefly ran third. Cooper missed the mid-season non-Championship races, which were useful pay-days for driver like Clark and Brabham, and while Bruce was third in the Italian GP, he was a lap down from Clark.

Jimmy Clark and his Lotus 25 were the main story of 1963, taking seven Championship races and five non-Championship events. He also came within a whisker of winning the Indianapolis 500 in his rookie year. It was ironic that Lotus covered itself in glory at the Brickyard while Cooper, the Indy pioneer, was absent.

Neither McLaren nor Maggs finished in the United States or Mexican races, but Bruce managed fourth in South Africa, a lap down. Bruce finished the season sixth in the World Championship while Cooper could manage only fifth in the Constructors' Cup behind Lotus, BRM, Brabham and Ferrari. Since Lotus and Brabham were also using Coventry Climax V8 engines, and Bruce was a proven driver, it was not difficult to pinpoint the reason.

Carroll Shelby bought two of the four Monaco Mk IVs made for the 1963 season and had fitted 4.7-litre Ford V8 engines. Thus he created the 'King Cobra' which was phenomenally successful in the States, though the credit tended to go to Shelby rather than Cooper. Considering its performance, the King Cobra was remarkably cheap (about $12,000 for a top-flight machine, ready to race) and soon American outfits like Dolphin and McKee Chevette were making cars along similar lines. From the exciting racing they provided, there would grow Can-Am.

For 1963, John Whitmore led the works Mini Cooper team with the second car driven by Timmy Mayer, who had won a 1962 Formula Junior Championship in America with a Cooper. When Mayer was not available, the second car was given to Paddy Hopkirk. Stuart Turner, BMC's competition manager, often put rally drivers in a third works Mini Cooper so that they could gain experience on tarmac. In all, twenty-one drivers raced works cars, some of them just the once, and they included Timo Makinen, Tony Fall and Rauno Altonen. Early in 1963, BMC announced the first Mini Cooper 'S' with a 1071cc engine, which enabled cars to compete on a more equal footing in categories with an 1100cc class. It was with such a car that Paddy Hopkirk and Henry Liddon would win the 1964 Monte Carlo Rally.

The rules of the British Saloon Car Championship gave points to the driver regardless of the car and at the last round in 1963, the title could have gone either to John Whitmore (Mini Cooper) or Jack Sears (7-litre Ford Galaxie and 1600cc Lotus-Cortina). Jack was able to use whichever car was best suited to the circuit and clinched the title by two points. In the new European Touring Car Championship, the Dutchman, Rob Slotemaker, won the 1300cc class in a Downton-tuned Mini Cooper.

In Formula Junior, Cooper took eight wins from the thirty-seven major races, but all were on the Continent without the presence of Arundell and his works Lotus. Though the BMC engine was giving 98bhp, it was well down on the Cosworth-Ford unit and Coopers were shown up on the faster circuits. Moreover, production of the FJ cars went down from twenty-eight (plus the Tyrrell cars) in 1962, to just 13 in 1963. It is not hard to see the reason why: Brabham sold eleven FJ cars in 1962,

Alec Issigonis with an enthusiastic Mini Cooper owner, Enzo Ferrari. Ferrari owned several Mini Coopers and was apt to take them for a blast on mountain roads whenever he needed to clear his mind.

twenty in 1963. Jack had not only weakened Cooper by leaving the team but, with Ron Tauranac, was in the process of destroying Cooper in the market-place.

Cooper was not finished, however, because 1964 saw Formula Junior replaced by Formula Three. Formula Junior had become a little too professional to fulfil its objective as a training category. Formula Three was intended to redress the balance by restricting capacity to 1000cc with just one carburettor, no more than four speeds in the gearbox and a minimum weight of 400kg. It was a rare sensible move by the governing body, since any existing FJ car could be adapted for the new Formula. In fact, the 1-litre 'screamer' Formula Three would pass into motor racing legend as one of the best categories ever. BMC produced a new short-stroke 970cc engine, which it offered in a road-going Mini Cooper 'S'. The company made parts for 1,000 cars so the unit could be homologated, but it is doubtful whether 1,000 road cars were completed. No matter, the 970cc engine was created so that Minis could win races and rallies.

The 1964 T72 Formula Three car used a spaceframe with a stressed aluminium skin and rocker arm inboard front suspension. Similar construction and layout were employed for the T71 Formula Two car and the T73 Formula One machine. Ken Tyrrell ran cars for Jackie Stewart and Warwick Banks. From twelve starts, Stewart took ten wins, including the prestigious support race to the Monaco Grand Prix. Banks was often a close second, and Warwick also won a race when Stewart had a clutch problem. Banks was overshadowed by Stewart, but part of the reason was

The works 997cc Mini Cooper with which John Love won the 1962 British Saloon Car Championship sits in the paddock at Snetterton before its first race. Behind is the sister car of John Whitmore. Note the standard steel wheels – apart from the racing numbers, and the absence of bumpers, this could be a shopping car.

The Monte Carlo Rally used to end with a number of tests including a thrash around the Monaco GP circuit. Paddy Hopkirk is seen doing this in his 997cc Mini Cooper in 1963, when he was sixth overall. The following year he would win outright in a 1071cc Cooper 'S'.

Conditions could be tough on the 'Monte' yet despite their 10-inch wheels, Mini Coopers were able to cope with deep snow. Actually 'cope' is the wrong word since Timo Makinen's Cooper 'S' is shown on its way to victory in the 1965 event. Conditions were so severe there were a mere 22 finishers from 237 starters.

that he was much taller and heavier than Stewart, which made a significant difference in small, light, cars producing perhaps 100bhp.

Cosworth Engineering was concentrating on Formula Two and it was left to Holbay Engineering to service most of the Ford runners. BMC, however, concentrated all its resources on the Tyrrell team. In all, eighteen T72s were made and though customers picked up the odd victory, when the Tyrrell twins did not win, the race tended to go to a Brabham.

Formula Two was revived in 1964 and the main parameter was that the engine should have no more than four cylinders and 1000cc. Cosworth produced the splendid SCA sohc engine, based on a Ford block and, before long, virtually everyone was using it. BMC attempted to make a bespoke Formula Two engine, but it proved woefully underpowered in testing and was never used.

The engine advantage that the Cooper works team enjoyed in Formula Three was therefore not available in Formula Two and the only win Cooper took was when Tony Hegbourne won the Grosser Preis von Berlin on the ultra-fast Avus track. Brabham took nine of the eighteen races, Lotus won seven, and Lola and Cooper picked up one apiece. Cooper was well-beaten, but then they sold only three F2 cars to the seventeen that Brabham sold.

LOSING THE RACE

During the winter of 1963/64, Owen Maddock had left Cooper to turn freelance and the first car he designed was the McLaren M1, a Group 7 sports car that used either a 4.5-litre Oldsmobile engine or a 4.7-litre Ford unit. It was the first car to bear Bruce's name and the first step towards what would become McLaren domination in 'big banger' sports car racing. Production was undertaken by Trojan, which had bought Elva, and twenty-four 'McLaren-Elvas' were made in 1964/5. By contrast, just nine Cooper Monacos were made after December 1963 and all but one went to America minus engines and gearboxes – six going to Shelby to be turned into King Cobras.

In Britain, Tommy Atkins bought a special Monaco Mk IV (T61P) and fitted it with a 5-litre Maserati V8 'quad cam' engine. Its usual driver was Roy Salvadori, in his last season of competition before becoming Cooper's team manager. It was a disappointment, however, not least because it produced nowhere near the 430bhp that Maserati claimed. It was the last sports car that Cooper made.

Although Coopers and Cooper-clones were doing very well in American sports car racing, Charlie Cooper refused to believe there was a viable market there and so Cooper missed its chance of the sharing the cash bonanza which was Can-Am racing.

Meanwhile the British Saloon Car Championship had revised rules for 1964 with the smallest class being for cars of 1300cc. John Cooper persuaded the works to make a road car with a 1275cc engine and this became the ultimate Mini Cooper road car. It was the 1275 'S', which starred in the movie, *The Italian Job* and which

In his last year of motor racing, Roy Salvadori handled a Cooper Monaco fitted with a 4.5-litre 'quad cam' Maserati V8 engine. On paper it should have been a winner – Roy was the most successful driver of a Monaco – but a number horses seem to have escaped on the journey from Italy to England.

135

The most successful Mini racer was John Rhodes, whom Jackie Stewart acknowledged was as quick as he was, but not as consistent. John earned the name Smokin' Rhodes and the reason is plain to see.

coachbuilders like Harold Radford and Wood & Pickett customised for wealthy customers. It was also the 1275 'S' that the Cooper works team ran in the 1964 British Saloon Car Championship, though they used wider bores with bigger pistons to give a capacity of 1293cc and, in race trim, about 110–112bhp. The main drivers were John Fitzpatrick and Paddy Hopkirk. 'Fitz' duly won the 1300cc class from Hopkirk and, overall, he was a close second to Jim Clark's Lotus-Cortina.

Warwick Banks in a 970cc Tyrrell car won the 1964 European Touring Car Championship outright. 1964 was the Mini Cooper's finest season in racing.

During 1964, Dunlop introduced a new tyre for the Mini, the CR48, which used F1 technology. The CR48 had a wider and fatter profile than standard rubber; it generated less heat and allowed the use of lower pressures. Tyres were beginning to become a crucial factor in all forms of motor racing whereas only three or four years previously there had been little difference between the tyres which Dunlop, say, had made for Formula One and for high-powered road sports cars.

Leaving Cooper's Formula One team, Tony Maggs joined the Scuderia Centro Sud, which was running BRMs, and Bruce was joined by Phil Hill who had wasted 1963 with the incompetent ATS team. The season started well enough with Bruce taking third in a rain-drenched *Daily Mirror* Trophy at Snetterton, but he was way off the pace at Goodwood where he was taken off by a spinning car.

McLaren qualified fifth for the Aintree 200, 2 seconds off the pace but, more worryingly, Phil Hill was 4.2 seconds adrift of pole. It was the first indication that 1964 was going to be a miserable season for the American. Phil is rare among racing drivers in that he is a cultivated man of great sensitivity. He was also a driver who liked the large canvas: give him a powerful car and a demanding circuit and he shone. Phil won nine races counting towards the World Sports Car Championship between 1953 and 1961 and only Stirling Moss won more. Hill simply was not suited temperamentally to cope with a team in decline.

As reigning World Champion constructor, Cooper was the first team to receive a Coventry Climax V8 engine in 1961. By 1964, Climax was giving its best attention to Lotus and Brabham, and it showed in the results. Phil managed fourth in the

International Trophy, but was a lap down. Neither car finished at Monaco and both were a long way adrift in the Dutch GP. McLaren finished second in Belgium, but only after both Dan Gurney's Brabham and Graham Hill's BRM had run out of fuel on the last lap. Had Bruce had another half gallon on board, he would have won, but he too ran dry within sight of the finish and Jim Clark pipped him.

Bruce and Phil were sixth and seventh – and lapped – in the French GP and Hill survived to take sixth in the British GP, two laps down. Both drivers had engines break at the Nürburgring and neither finished in Austria. Phil missed the Italian GP as he recovered from the effects of a crash and his stand-in, John Love, failed to qualify, but Bruce was a splendid second after one of those slip-streaming epics that were a feature of Monza before chicanes were introduced.

That was the last time that a works Cooper scored points in 1964. Bruce finished the year seventh in the Drivers' Championship (won by John Surtees) while Phil was equal seventeenth with a single point. In the Constructors' Cup, won by Ferrari, Cooper was fifth beating only the British Racing Partnership which was running copies of the Lotus 25 with rather breathless customer BRM engines.

1964 had been a miserable season during which John Cooper had nearly lost his life. John and BMC had each been developing a twin-engined Mini Cooper. They were not the first; Paul Emery and Chris Lawrence had both attempted the exercise without success. John says:

I thought that, if we could make it work, it could be a fantastic rally car, four-wheel-drive years before the Audi quattro. BMC had made a twin-engined version of the Mini Moke which it hoped to sell to the army and it worked splendidly in trials. Our car used a Mini front subframe bolted at the back with the steering arms welded up. The gearboxes were linked to one change, but there was no other connection between the two units. We didn't have an interlinking differential, we just let nature take its course, front to rear, and it worked. Our drivers loved it and I believe to this day that the concept had fantastic potential. I was driving it along the Kingston bypass when one of the welded steering arms at the rear came adrift. . . .

John was very seriously injured and BMC, which had run its twin-engined car in practice for the Targa Florio (it didn't start because one of the engines blew), immediately knocked its project on the head. Further, it let it be known that it disapproved of any further experimentation with twin-engined cars.

John's absence from the team for much of the Grand Prix season did not help the Cooper cause. Then, in October 1964, Charlie Cooper died suddenly of a heart attack. Irascible he may have been, and not infrequently wrong in major decisions he made in the 1960s, but Charlie had made Cooper Cars into a sensible business, the first time that any maker of single-seater racing cars had done so.

Roy Salvadori was drafted in as team manager for 1965 and, through Roy, an introduction was made to Jonathan Sieff. Jonathan had raced until a serious accident during practice for Le Mans in 1960. He was head of the Chipstead Motor Group and a member of the family that controlled Marks & Spencer. In April 1965, Cooper Cars became part of the Chipstead Motor Group and there was some talk of sponsorship from Marks & Spencer even though 'on car' sponsors would not arrive

Bruce McLaren's T73 at the 1964 British GP. By then Cooper was low in the pecking order for Coventry Climax engines, but Bruce still qualified a splendid sixth. He was lying fifth when on lap 8, the normally reliable Cooper/Jack Knight six-speed gearbox failed.

until 1968. John Cooper remained with Cooper Cars on a service contract and those who were at Cooper during this period are of the opinion that John became increasingly marginalised. Old hands were confused by the number of new faces that appeared at the factory, men in suits who appeared to have no purpose and no idea about the realities of racing.

In Formula One, Bruce was joined by Jochen Rindt, who had enjoyed a sensational début season in Formula Two. Jochen would emerge as the quickest Formula One driver of his generation, but one would not have known that from his 1965 season. Understandably enough, he was slower than Bruce at first as he learned the ropes. Bruce, in turn, was typically slower than the entries from Lotus, BRM, Brabham, Ferrari and, often, the two Brabhams entered by Rob Walker. Bruce took fifth in the South African Grand Prix and in the Race of Champions at Brands Hatch, fourth at the Easter Monday Goodwood meeting and sixth in the International Trophy – and on each occasion he was a lap down.

At Monaco Bruce was fifth, two laps down. Third in the Belgian GP appears good on paper, but he was 5.9 seconds off the pace in qualifying and again he was lapped. Neither Cooper driver finished in the points in France, Britain or Holland, but Jochen scored his first World Championship points with fourth place in the German GP. There were, however, only eight finishers and Jochen had been 14.8 seconds off pole in qualifying.

McLaren picked up fifth in Italy, a lap down, Rindt was sixth in the United States GP, two laps down, and neither finished in Mexico. Bruce ended the year ninth in the World Championship with ten points, while Jochen's four points gave him thirteenth. Cooper was fifth in the Constructors' Cup, a bare three points ahead of Honda in its first full season. At the end of the season, Bruce left Cooper to concentrate on his own team.

In Formula Two, Rindt drove a Brabham for Roy Winkelmann Racing and finished second to Clark in the French F2 Championship. The best finish by a Cooper was Stewart's second place at Oulton Park in early April. No Cooper finished higher than fifth in any other race.

Still on the theme of special bodies, this unusual car, driven by Bill Elmes in a 1966 hill climb, began life at a T39 Manx Tail sports car. The car has a different body and the driver has been moved from the centre to a more conventional position on the right.

Believe it or not, beneath the striking and unusual body there lurks a Cooper Monaco. In 1966 people were still maintaining the honourable tradition of taking a Cooper and modifying it to their own requirements.

Bruce McLaren and his T66 testing at a deserted Goodwood in April 1964 with John Cooper operating the watches. Goodwood was the favoured test circuit of most British teams since it offered a wide variety of corners and, in Cooper's case, was less than 90 minutes drive from the factory.

On the back of Jackie Stewart's storming Formula Three season in 1964, Cooper had sold nineteen Formula Three cars. Between them they managed three wins from the sixty-one F3 races held in Europe in 1965.

For the first time in years there was no Cooper sports car, yet sports car racing was burgeoning on both sides of the Atlantic. The irony is that the Xerox Special and the Cooper Monaco-based King Cobras played a fundamental rôle in popularising the category. Just as Cooper had stormed Indianapolis, but never returned, so it missed the boat in what would become a very lucrative market where McLaren was doing particularly well with cars designed by Owen Maddock.

The only bright spot of 1965 was the performance of the Mini Cooper 1275 'S'. It had been developed to allow Cooper to exploit the 1300cc class in racing but, in 1965, it became the first car in history to win seven major international rallies in a single season. In the British Saloon Car Championship, Warwick Banks was joined in the works team by John Rhodes. Banks won the 1000cc class, and was runner-up overall in the Championship. He might have taken the title outright but for the fact he was shunted from behind in a race at Crystal Palace. Rhodes, then thirty-eight and a latecomer to racing, took the 1300cc class, and would do so again, and again. John had a knack of making a demon start and his car would be swathed in smoke at the first corner as he used his front tyres to scrub off speed. It earned him the nickname, 'Smokin'' Rhodes.

Apart from the continuing success of the Mini Coopers, the one cause for optimism was the forthcoming 3-litre Formula One, due to take effect from 1966. Thanks to Mario Tozzi-Condivi, Cooper was able to strike a deal with Maserati for the supply of engines. Tozzi-Condivi was a co-founder of the Chipstead Motor Group, a long-time friend of Roy Salvadori, and an ace salesman with unequalled contacts in Italy. Lotus and BRM would have to start 1966 with 2-litre versions of their existing V8s, Ferrari would use a modified sports car engine, while McLaren was still looking for a suitable engine. The Maserati deal, therefore, appeared to have the potential to put Cooper back on top. The team faced 1966 with more confidence than it had enjoyed for some time.

CHAPTER TEN

INDIAN SUMMER

The 60° Maserati V12 engine had first appeared in 1957. One had been used in a sports car chassis, and run in the Mille Miglia, and another had run in the Italian Grand Prix. On both occasions the drivers found that though the engine was powerful (320bhp was claimed), the torque band was narrow. At the end of 1957 Maserati withdrew from racing so the potential of the V12 remained unexplored, though it was dusted off again for some sports car racing in 1961. For 1966 Guilio Alfieri, Maserati's brilliant chief designer, revived his old design. He shortened the stroke, increased the bore, and turned a 2.5-litre engine into a 3-litre unit with Lucas fuel injection and a coil for each spark plug.

Cooper Cars underwrote the development of the engine and, in return, received works engines on loan plus the UK franchise for the unit. By mid-season it was claimed to give 360bhp, which compares with a claimed 375bhp for Ferrari's V12 and a rock-solid 310bhp for the Repco V8 used by Brabham. BRM was to claim up to 420bhp for its horrendously complicated H16 unit but, since it rarely finished a race, that was of academic interest only.

John Surtees still had not developed the Cooper-Maserati to his liking at the 1966 British GP. John was running fifth before transmission trouble developed, but he had made the car into a winner by the end of the season.

141

Jochen Rindt, who became the sport's only posthumous World Champion in 1970, sits in his Cooper-Maserati before the 1967 German GP. He retired with engine trouble, which was an all too familiar a story that year.

Leading hill climber, Roy Lane, is on flat ground at the August 1967 Kimble Sprint. The engine appears to be a highly modified 1498cc Ford unit, and is another instance of the many and varied uses to which Coopers were put.

Derrick White, Cooper's new chief designer, and later a leading figure in CART racing in the States, designed Cooper's first monocoque chassis. Suspension of the T81 followed previous Cooper practice, but an innovation was the mounting of the front disc brakes on stub axles from the wheels so they were in the airstream. With each of the side pontoons carrying 114 litres of fuel (the V12 was thirsty) the resulting car was not lissome.

Initially, the works ran cars for Jochen Rindt and Richie Ginther but, for the first time in years, Cooper sold Formula One cars to privateers. Jo Bonnier and Guy Ligier each had a T81 while Rob Walker ran Jo Siffert in the spaceframe T80 'mule' in the International Trophy before taking delivery of a T81. Brabham won the International Trophy from Surtees and Bonnier, but Rindt had demonstrated the new car's potential by qualifying third. No Cooper finished at Monaco, where they lacked the nimbleness to go well, but Rindt qualified and finished second in the Belgian GP.

Surtees won in Belgium but a difference of opinion with the Ferrari team manager, Eugenio Dragoni, led to his departure. Had sense prevailed, and it was Dragoni who was shown the door, it is likely that Surtees would have won Championships for Ferrari in 1966 and 1967. Mario Tozzi-Condivi was the first person outside of the Ferrari team to hear the news and he got his co-directors out of bed and held a meeting at five in the morning. The upshot was that they agreed to build a new car and let it be known that they had a car waiting for the right driver. Surtees was soon on the phone.

Surtees qualified second in the French GP at Reims, but the torrid heat gave Cooper problems with engine cooling and fuel vaporisation. Ginther had been recalled by Honda and thereafter the third Cooper was used by a number of drivers, including Chris Amon at Reims.

BRABHAM DOMINATION

France saw Jack Brabham become the first man to win a Grand Prix in a car of his own construction – actually, he was a 50/50 partner with Ron Tauranac – while the only Cooper to finish was that of Rindt, in fourth place and lapped twice. Surtees and Rindt could qualify no higher than sixth and seventh for the British GP at Brands Hatch, slower than Dan Gurney whose Eagle was still fitted with an old four-cylinder 2.7-litre Coventry Climax FPF unit. Rindt finished fifth.

The best Cooper performance in the Dutch GP was Bonnier in seventh, and lapped six times. Surtees' influence on the team showed at the Nürburgring when, with a well-sorted car, he qualified second to Clark's 2-litre Lotus-Climax. Brabham won his fourth race in a row, but Surtees and Rindt came home second and third. Rindt took fourth at Monza, then second in the United States GP, with Surtees third and Siffert fourth. Finally Surtees ended his spell with Cooper by winning in Mexico. It was no fluke. John set pole but was slow away and lay fifth after the first lap. By lap 6 he was in the lead and he stayed there until the end. John had developed a problematic car into a race winner. He then accepted an invitation from Honda to both drive and to control the UK end of the operation. His win in Mexico was Cooper's only single-seater victory in 1966.

After years of loyally supporting Cooper, Ken Tyrrell had seen the writing on the wall and had switched to new French Matra chassis for Formula Two. Cooper made just two Formula Two cars (T82) and neither was successful even though they were driven by Bob Anderson (an excellent F1 privateer) and Jo Siffert. After a handful of races, they both switched chassis. Brabham-Hondas won all but one F2 race – and that was won by a Brabham-Cosworth. Brabham had struggled with an earlier Honda engine during 1965, and Jack and Ron Tauranac had flown to Japan to teach Honda how to make an engine that would work in a car and not just on a test rig.

John Rhodes and Warwick Banks savour their victory in a three-hour race at Mallory Park in 1964. That year Banks enjoyed success driving a Formula Three Cooper-BMC for Ken Tyrrell – with Jackie Stewart as his team-mate. Banks also won the European Touring Car Championship in a 970cc Cooper 'S' entered by Tyrrell.

Lord Snowdon is given the low-down on the Mini Cooper 'S' that won the 1965 Monte Carlo Rally crewed by Timo Makinen and Paul Easter. Snowdon, then married to Princess Margaret and a fashionable photographer in his own right, was one of the celebrities who gave the Mini Cooper matchless social cachet.

For Formula Three, Cooper made just seven cars while Brabham made fifty-six and dominated. In 1965, Ford-engined Coopers had generally been more successful than those with BMC units. At the end of 1965, BMC gave up supplying racing engines and so, in its last year in Formula Three, Cooper used Ford-based units. The Cooper T83 looked the business, being notably sleek, but it suffered from extreme understeer caused by front-end lift. Few people knew much about racing car aerodynamics at the time and those who did were not free with the information. It was years later that Cooper realised where the problem lay but, in 1966, the team had to watch the 1965 model out-perform the new car.

Mini Coopers filled the top three places in the 1966 Monte Carlo Rally, with Paddy Hopkirk first – then they were disqualified over a technical infringement. A Citroën was promoted to first, to its crew's embarrassment. It was blatant bias by the French who had changed the class structure to favour near-standard Group 1 cars – 5,000 had to be built in the previous year and the 1275 'S' had achieved only about half that in 1964. After BMC's competition manager, Stuart Turner, read the rules and spoke to his bosses, production of the Mini Cooper in 1965 reached the target so it was eligible for the 1966 Monte Carlo Rally.

The disqualification back-fired on the French because the incident made headlines round the world and everyone remembers that the Minis were so good that they had to be nobbled whereas you have to be petrolhead to remember who was awarded the win. The 'winning' Mini Cooper made a star appearance at the end of the popular television show, *Sunday Night At The London Palladium*. The band played 'Rule Britannia' and the audience stood and joined in. Any Frenchman there would have been wise to have claimed to be Belgian.

Mini Coopers went on to win outright five international rallies where they merely faced top-class opponents and not French organisers. But in racing, the Mini Cooper

1967 was the last year that Mini Coopers regularly took outright wins in international rallies. That year the Monte was won by Rauno Aaltonen and Henry Liddon in a 1275cc Cooper 'S' while team-mates, and winners of the 1965 event, Timo Makinen and Paul Easter were forced to retire.

was starting to feel its age and tyres were the problem; with 10-inch wheels, a driver could destroy a set in seven or eight laps. Dunlop produced new compounds and patterns and the works cars ran 5.75J tyres at the front, 4.5Js at the rear. Smokin' Rhodes again won the 1300cc class in the British Saloon Car Championship, but the title went to John Fitzpatrick in a Broadspeed Ford Anglia.

For 1967 Rindt was paired with Pedro Rodriguez in the works F1 team; Pedro qualified third for the South African GP and won it. It was, however, a lucky win because, with six laps to go, he was second to John Love in a Cooper T79 fitted with a 2.7-litre Coventry Climax FPF engine. Love led by a country mile when he had to stop to take on a couple of gallons of fuel. It was nearly the biggest upset in Grand Prix history since Nuvolari beat Auto Union and Mercedes-Benz in the 1935 German GP, but Love did finish second. Cooper, therefore, scored its first 1–2 in a World Championship race since the heady days of 1960 – and Rodriguez and Love lapped the other finishers at least once.

In the Race of Champions at Brands Hatch, only one of the four Coopers finished – Rodriguez in fourth. Siffert managed a strong third place in the International Trophy and Rodriguez was a distant fifth at Monaco. Neither Rindt nor Rodriguez finished in Holland though they qualified fourth and fifth. Rindt was fourth in Belgium, and Siffert was fourth, with Rodriguez fifth in the British GP. Given the quality of the drivers using Cooper-Maseratis, these were poor results, but Cooper had simply not kept pace with the opposition. For a start, the claimed 360bhp from the engine must be regarded with scepticism, as must all Italian claims of the period.

Then Lotus had taken delivery of the first Cosworth DFV engines and had won first time out in Holland. Not only did Lotus have exclusive use of what would be the

For the 1968 British Saloon Car Championship the works Mini Coopers had fuel injection. By then they had also acquired much wider wheels as the add-on flared wheel arch indicates.

most successful engine in motor racing history, but the Lotus 49 that used it marked a revolution in chassis design. Ferrari had increased its power to a claimed 408bhp and Brabham had a completely new Repco V8.

In the meantime, Cooper had more or less stood still. A 'lightweight' car, the T86, appeared at the British GP for Rindt, and it raced four times, failing to finish on each occasion. Bonnier and Ligier were a distant fifth and sixth in Germany, the best finish in Canada was Bonnier in eighth and five laps down, while Rindt inherited fourth at Monza. Siffert was fourth in America and Rodriguez was sixth in his home Grand Prix, Mexico.

The drivers' championship was won by Denny Hulme, from team boss Jack Brabham, and the highest Cooper driver was Rodriguez in seventh. Brabham won the constructors' title easily from Lotus with Cooper third, ahead of Ferrari, Honda, BRM, Eagle and Honda. That sounds better than it actually was. Almost half of Cooper's score had come from the win in South Africa when it was basically the best of the 1966 cars. After that, Cooper's highest finish had been fourth, as rival teams introduced 1967 cars, and Cooper had also had the advantage of private cars in the capable hands of Bonnier and Siffert.

A single T84 F2 car was made for 1967. It was slimmer than its predecessor and had similar front brakes to the F1 car. Peter Gethin managed to place it third in a minor race at Hockenheim, but that was due more to Gethin's skill than anything else. It was not a quality field.

It seems that two T85 F3 cars were built, but there is no record of them ever racing. Cooper, which had once been the largest maker of single-seaters in the world, was out of the production racing car market altogether.

Mini Coopers won seven major rallies in 1967, including a third (fourth?) 'Monte', but it would be the last year that the cars were capable of taking outright

Mini Coopers won the Monte Carlo Rally three times – four if you count the time that the organisers turned somersaults to find ways of disqualifying them. By 1968, when Tony Fall and Mike Wood were crewing this car, Mini Coopers were having to settle for class wins rather than outright victory in international rallies.

wins on a regular basis. They still took class wins, but a new generation of cars, led by special editions of the Ford Escort, took charge of the sharp end of the field.

For the 1967 British Saloon Car Championship, the works Mini Coopers received fuel injection. John Rhodes, backed by John Handley, won the 1300cc class yet again, and came close to Frank Gardner's Ford Falcon for the overall title.

Minis raced under a handicap because cars such as the Ford Anglia, with 13-inch wheels, could benefit from tyres developed for Formula Two and Three whereas Minis had to have tyres developed specially for them and there was not the same edge of competition as in single-seater racing.

STUCK IN FIRST GEAR

Cooper began the 1968 Formula One season with Maserati-engined cars for Brian Redman and Ludovico Scarfiotti and Bonnier and Siffert soldiered on with their 1966 cars. Rindt had gone to Brabham and Rodriguez to BRM. The best performance in qualifying for the South African GP was Scarfiotti, fifteenth on the grid and 4.7 seconds off the pace. Only Siffert finished – seventh and three laps down. It was the last time that a Maserati engine appeared in a World Championship race.

By the time the Race of Champions was run three months later, Siffert had a Lotus 49 and Bonnier a McLaren-BRM, so Cooper's presence on the grid was seriously diminished. Cooper had switched to a BRM unit – a V12 originally intended for use in sports cars. It would be developed into a race winner but, in 1968, it was probably the least powerful engine in F1. Moreover, whereas Lotus previously had exclusive use of the Cosworth DFV, in 1968 the unit was supplied to Tyrrell, running Matra chassis, and McLaren. All but one round of the World

Chris Lawrence, better known for his exploits with Morgans, drove this private Cooper T71 fitted with an engine from a Ferrari 250GTO in a couple of Grands Prix in 1966. In the British GP at Brands Hatch he finished eleventh and last, seven laps down.

Another shot of Chris Lawrence's T71 Cooper-Ferrari, which makes an interesting comparison with the T81 Cooper-Maserati below.

Guy Ligier, former French rugby international, drove his own Cooper-Maserati T81 during 1966. He is pictured in the British GP at Brands Hatch where he finished tenth. Ligier later established his own F1 team which had an uneven history for twenty years before being taken over by Alain Prost.

Jo 'last of the late brakers' Siffert in Rob Walker's Cooper-Maserati T81 at the 1961 British GP. Jo was out of the running on this occasion but, two years later, would win at Brands Hatch in Walker's Lotus 72.

Australian all-rounder, and wit and raconteur, Frank Gardner, had an outing in a works Cooper-BRM T86B in the 1968 International Trophy. A cylinder liner cracked at half distance.

Brian Redman in a works Cooper-BRM T86B on his way to fifth place in the 1968 Race of Champions at Brands Hatch. Brian was much in demand as a Formula One driver, but he didn't like the atmosphere of F1 and spent most of his career in sports cars.

Championship would be won by a Cosworth-powered car and the three Cosworth teams would fill the top three places of the Constructors' Cup. A new era of Formula One had begun.

At Brands Hatch Redman had a T86B, a slimmer development of the unsuccessful 1967 'lightweight' car. But it was lightweight only by comparison to other Coopers, it was not light by Lotus or Matra standards. Redman inherited fifth in the Race of Champions, then Frank Gardner had the car for the International Trophy, but a cylinder liner cracked at one-third distance. Redman and Scarfiotti were third and fourth in the Spanish GP, but they were the last healthy runners – they'd occupied the last two places on the grid. Scarfiotti was fourth at Monaco, but only because he finished. He had started from last place.

By the end of the next race, the Belgian GP, Cooper was in real trouble. Scarfiotti, a man who had a Grand Prix win for Ferrari under his belt, had been killed while practising for a round of the European Hill Climb Championship. His replacement, the Belgian, Lucien Bianchi, was no more than a journeyman, but he did come sixth at Spa simply because he finished. During the race Redman crashed and broke an arm when a front wishbone snapped. A breakage on a Cooper was almost unheard of, but the values that John Cooper, Jack Brabham, Bruce McLaren and Owen Maddock had applied to everything they did had been eroded.

Bianchi crashed the sole Cooper in Holland and the French GP saw two new drivers: former rally star, Vic Elford, and the rising Frenchman, Johnny Servoz-Gavin. Johnny crashed, but Vic eventually inherited fourth place.

Bianchi was entered for the British GP, Elford kept his drive, and a third car was entered for Robin Widdows. Bianchi's car wasn't ready, Elford and Widdows had only two cars, both privateers, behind them on the grid and neither Cooper finished. Elford and Bianchi turned up for the German GP, but they might as well not have bothered. While Jackie Stewart put in one of the greatest drives in history in wet and misty conditions, Elford crashed on lap 1 and Bianchi had a fuel leak. Only Elford started in the Italian GP – and crashed on lap 3. Vic then finished fifth in Canada, four laps down, and that was the last occasion that a Cooper won World Championship points. Elford had a private entry in a T86B-BRM in the 1969 International Trophy and Monaco GP and both times he was last finisher, many laps behind.

There were no cars from Cooper for Formula Two or Three in 1968 but, for 1969, there was the T90 for Formula 5000. The Cooper management boasted that a production run of twenty-four had been laid down and predicted success on both sides of the Atlantic. In fact, just two were made and they were both failures.

In June 1969, the effects of Cooper Cars were sold. The only bright spot of the year was that Smokin Rhodes won the 1300cc class in the British Saloon Car Championship and, in a private car, Gordon Spice won the 1000cc class.

The 1968 European Touring Car Championship was run on a class-by-class basis with no overall Champion. John Handley in a BMC-supported private car won the 1000cc class and John Rhodes won the 1600cc class in his 1300cc works Mini. It was the Mini Cooper's swansong in international racing and was, perhaps, its finest hour.

By the end of 1968, not only was Cooper Cars all but finished, but BMC had begun the process of takeovers and mergers that was to take it close to oblivion. Support for Cooper's Mini Cooper team was an early casualty and the company ran its own 1275cc cars for John Rhodes and John Handley. Unfortunately, the Abingdon competition department had been geared for rallies and long-distance races, not sprints. A team demoralised by the threat of the axe never did get to grips with the problem.

Vic Elford with the Cooper-BRM T86B at Brands Hatch in the 1968 British GP. Vic remains the only driver to graduate to Formula One from the world of rallying – earlier that year he had won the Monte Carlo Rally for Porsche. At Brands Hatch, however, his engine let go on lap 27.

Curse you, Red Baron! F1 cars sprouted high mounted wings during 1968 and Vic Elford couldn't help sending the whole business up.

Another example of the way Coopers often had an afterlife. Peter Hawtin's T86B enters Bottom Bend at Brands Hatch in a club event in 1970.

John Cooper obtained sponsorship from Britax, the seat-belt maker, to field his own Mini Coopers. Daniel Richmond prepared the engines and Ginger Devlin continued to run the team. The drivers were Steve Neal and Gordon Spice and 12-inch wheels were adopted. The sensible thing would have been to run in the 1000cc class, but Cooper's drivers wanted to take on the Abingdon works team. So the two top Mini teams contested the 1300cc class with the result they took points from each other, which allowed Chris Craft in a Broadspeed Escort to take the class and finish runner-up overall. The championship was won by Alec Poole's private Mini Cooper running in the 1000cc class. The 1969 Britax Mini Cooper effort was the last team with which John Cooper, or Cooper Cars, was associated.

Soon afterwards, Sir Donald Stokes, head of the British Leyland Motor Corporation severed links with both John Cooper and Donald Healey. One reason was that he objected to paying them the modest royalty they received for every car that bore their names. Britain's largest motor company was run by a 'super salesman' who was the only man in the world who did not understand that an Austin-Healey Sprite had more appeal than an Austin Sprite and that a Mini Cooper was more glamorous than a Mini Clubman. Stokes severed the link with Cooper just after the film, *The Italian Job*, had made the Mini Cooper an international star to tens of millions of people who knew nothing of the exploits of Paddy Hopkirk or John Rhodes. For his valuable contribution to British industry, Stokes was later elevated to the peerage.

With the scrapping of the agreement with Cooper went plans for 'Cooper' versions of other BLMC saloons, including the 1800 'land crab'. Cooper Cars became a successful string of BMW dealerships. John Cooper himself moved to the south coast and started John Cooper Garages. The new business sold Hondas.

EPILOGUE

For many years John Cooper lived in relative obscurity. His new business, run with the integrity which had marked all his dealings, prospered. But Mini Coopers continued to race. Three World Champions – Niki Lauda, James Hunt and Alan Jones – all began their careers in one. The Mini Se7en and Mini Miglia championships gave many a driver a chance to go racing and some graduated to the higher echelons of saloon car racing. Richard Longman, for instance, won the British Saloon Car Championship outright in 1978 and 1979 in a highly modified Clubman GTs, and the Clubman GT incorporated the main elements of the Mini Cooper.

As Historic racing grew in popularity, John emerged again into the limelight. Then, in the early 1980s, British Leyland discovered that much of the British public thought that the Mini had ceased production but, if it was available, they'd consider buying one. That led to an aggressive marketing campaign and the Mini, particularly the Cooper models, became a cult in Japan. Japanese enthusiasts began to import Mini Coopers, which now had 'classic' status.

Meanwhile, John and his son Mike had been playing around with Minis, and Metros, with a view to making a Cooper for the 1980s. Then Rover Japan commissioned John to build a new 1275cc Mini Cooper. The Coopers installed an engine from an MG Metro and it was shipped to Japan. Rover Japan was very enthusiastic and wanted 1,000 cars, but the parent company was indifferent. With that line blocked, Rover Japan suggested a Cooper kit. For the 998cc car, John and Mike came up with a twin-carburettor conversion, with a modified cylinder head and the name 'Cooper' prominent. More than 1,000 kits were sold in Japan and Rover Group took notice. The company entered talks with John and Mike and agreed to market the Cooper Conversion, with full warranty, through its dealer network.

To mark the thirtieth anniversary of the Mini, in 1989, Rover launched a Special Edition with a white roof, the twin-carburettor conversion kit, and copies of the Cooper racing wheels. The following year came a 1275cc car, first with a single carburettor, which had white stripes on the bonnet with John's signature on them. In parallel, John Cooper Garages made a twin-carb kit that was essentially the 'S' version. Rover intended to make just 1,000 cars, but they sold out in the first week. It was decided to reintroduce the Mini Cooper as a regular production model.

From 1991, the engine was fitted with single-point fuel injection and a catalytic converter and John Cooper Garages made a limited edition (of thirty-five cars) called the 'Grand Prix'. After that, Cooper diversified: customers could buy performance kits, sweatshirts, Cooper wheelnuts and gear knobs, a 1400cc engine – just about anything, including air conditioning, a television and a fridge. Basically, if something could be fitted into a car, a customer could have it and one wealthy enthusiast handed over £34,000 for a Mini Cooper that had everything. In addition, Jack Knight Developments, so closely associated with Cooper Cars in its days in racing, produced a range of equipment including a five-speed gearbox in road and race

Second coming – this revived Mini Cooper of the 1990s is decked out with extra lights to recall the days when Mini Coopers dominated rallying.

forms, a six-speed gearbox for racing and a 16-valve dohc cylinder head. These were particularly popular in Japan which had become the Mini's main market – larger even than Britain.

In 1994 BMW took over the Rover Group, then owned by British Aerospace but, unlike Donald Stokes, the new boss, Bernd Pichetsrieder, had an acute sense of heritage and history – he was the nephew of Sir Alec Issigonis. In 1996, a new Mini Cooper was launched with two-point fuel injection, air bags, side-impact bars and the radiator was at the front, not the side. The new car was softer than the old 1275 'S' with a plusher interior. Power, top speed and acceleration were all down on the 1275 'S', but it still found buyers by the thousand.

In 1997, BMW showed its replacement for the Mini, to be produced from 2000 with a new 1600cc engine made in conjunction with Chrysler. The announcement

James Hunt with John Cooper at Brands Hatch in 1976. Hunt was one of three World Champions (with Niki Lauda and Alan Jones) to start his career in racing with a Mini Cooper.

emphasised that Cooper and Cooper 'S' versions would be included in the range. Indeed, John had been consulted over the new design and was one of the few people to drive the prototype.

It is ironic that the Cooper name is better known today than it was when Cooper was winning World Championships and dominating Formula Two. John, the modest man of Formula One, now enjoys greater celebrity among more people than ever before. It is not due only to the revival of the Mini Cooper; Cooper racing and sports cars are stars in Historic race meetings all over the world. A new generation of enthusiasts know about John Cooper and an older generation has never forgotten him, nor his huge contribution to the British motor racing renaissance.

In the late 1960s, the perception of Cooper was that of a failing company. More then thirty years on, John and Charlie Cooper's considerable achievements can be seen in perspective. Between 1948 and the early 1960s they made more single-seater racing cars, and provided opportunities for more rising stars to shine than any previous maker in history – and more than most of the outfits that have followed in their footsteps.

INDEX